Conflicts and Challenges in Early Christianity

Conflicts and Challenges in Early Christianity

Martin Hengel
and C.K. Barrett

Edited by
Donald A. Hagner

TRINITY PRESS INTERNATIONAL
Harrisburg, Pennsylvania

Trinity Press International, P.O. Box 1321, Harrisburg, PA 17105
Trinity Press International is a division of the Morehouse Group.

Cover design: Trude Brummer

Library of Congress Cataloging-in-Publication Data

Conflicts and challenges in early Christianity / Martin Hengel, C. K. Barrett ; edited by Donald A. Hagner.
    p.   cm.
   Includes bibliographical references and index.
   Contents: Early Christianity as a Jewish-Messianic, universalistic movement / Martin Hengel – Paul, councils and controversies / C. K. Barrett.
   ISBN 1-56338-291-1 (pbk. alk. : paper)
   1. Jews in the New Testament. 2. Christianity and other religions – Judaism. 3. Judaism – Relations – Christianity. 4. Bible. N.T. – Criticism, interpretation, etc.   I. Hengel, Martin. Early Christianity as a Jewish-Messianic, universalistic movement. II. Barrett, C. K. (Charles Kingsley), 1917-   Paul, councils and controversies. III. Hagner, Donald Alfred.
BS2545.J44C65 1999
270.1 – dc21   99-36959

Printed in the United States of America

99 00 01 02 03 04   10 9 8 7 6 5 4 3 2 1

Contents

Preface

New Testament scholarship is or should be an exciting enterprise. The interest of the public and even the average seminarian, however, is nowadays sparked more often by conferences that focus on practical matters than on traditional academic discussions. The topics that quickly pack rooms with excited listeners are those oriented to success in ministry, to personal experience, to signs and wonders. The dichotomy is unfortunate and unjustified, for academic theology is the indispensable foundation and the lodestar of authentic ministry and fulfilling Christian experience.

To reawaken an enthusiasm for academic study of the New Testament, Fuller Theological Seminary's New Testament department instituted an annual colloquium in the spring of 1997. On that first occasion we were privileged to have Martin Hengel of Tübingen as our guest lecturer. At the 1998 colloquium we were honored by the presence of C. K. Barrett of Durham, England, as our lecturer. Both events occasioned an extraordinary excitement on our Pasadena campus. It was gratifying to see packed rooms for presentations of academic papers on the New Testament. To be sure, this was in large measure due to the exceptional prominence of our lecturers. Nevertheless this was an excitement for the academic study of the New Testament.

These seminal essays by two leading New Testament scholars focus on the interface between Judaism and Christianity in the New Testament. Professor Hengel writes in a broad and incisive manner on "Early Christianity as a Jewish-Messianic, Universalist Movement." He argues that Christianity grew out of Jewish soil and that pagan influences in the New Testament were mediated through Hellenistic Judaism. He contends accordingly, and with an increasing number of Jewish scholars, that the New Testament must be considered an important source for our knowledge of ancient Judaism. In the last section of the essay he comments in some detail on "the final separation" of Christianity and Judaism.

Professor Barrett's essay, "Paul: Councils and Controversies," addresses a more specific topic, but one with wide-ranging implications, namely, the council reflected in Galatians 2 and Acts 15. What is the gospel of Jesus Christ for the Jews and what is it for the Gentiles of the Pauline mission? He explores the historical circumstances and the theological issues at stake, tracing the weakness of the initial compromise agreement between Paul and Peter to take the gospel to the uncircumcision and the circumcision respectively, as well as the significance of the later, compromise decree of the council that made minimal demands upon the Gentiles. The inadequacy of both Jerusalem agreements is found in the failure to refer to the center of the gospel, Jesus Christ.

In both cases the main lectures were followed by responses and discussion from a panel made up of members of Fuller Seminary's New Testament department, as well as questions from the floor. Responding to Professor Hengel's lecture were Ralph P. Martin, distinguished scholar in residence and doyen of our department, and David M. Scholer and Seyoon Kim. Responding to Professor Barrett's lectures were again Professors Martin and Kim, together with G. Walter Hansen.

A brief final chapter in the present book draws together some of the themes of the two essays by summarizing the responses of these faculty members and the further comments of the lecturers. A few concluding paragraphs draw out the implications of the presentations and discussions for the future. Also provided is an annotated bibliography that includes items mentioned by the lecturers and panelists, as well as other books and articles especially pertinent to the themes of the two colloquia.

I want to thank first of all Professors Hengel and Barrett for accepting the invitation to be our New Testament colloquium lecturers and for making the colloquium such a wonderful event in each case. Second, I warmly thank my departmental colleagues for their enthusiastic participation in the panel discussions. And finally, I thank my graduate assistant, Chris Spinks, for his help in readying the manuscripts for publication and for preparing the Scripture index.

DONALD A. HAGNER

1
Early Christianity as a Jewish-Messianic, Universalistic Movement

Martin Hengel

The Relationship Between Judaism and Early Christianity

As I was preparing this essay, I noticed step by step that a series of Jewish scholars and scholars of antiquity have anticipated what I intend to say; unfortunately, their work has received far too little recognition and consideration, especially in my home country. In fact, given my topic and present audience, it may be that I am only bringing owls to Athens; so while I expect to meet with sharp criticism from other circles, here I will be presenting little more than a résumé of what is already familiar.

1. Today no Christian theologian would deny that Christianity began and took root in Jewish soil. But this consensus begins to become questionable, at least among many of my Protestant colleagues, if I add but one word and say without qualification that Christianity grew *entirely* out of Jewish soil. By arguing that early Christianity is completely a child of Judaism I am going against the view that early Christianity is a syncretistic religion with various roots, a view that was originally formulated by Hermann Gunkel, subsequently accepted in the German school of religious history at the end of the nineteenth century, and firmly established in New Testament scholarship due to the influence of Rudolf Bultmann.

Translated by John R. Betz.

As the argument goes, Judaism was not alone at the cradle of Christianity but was attended by such diverse godfathers as Gnosticism, Greek and Oriental mysteries, magic, astrology, pagan polytheism, stories of divine men (*theioi andres*) and their miraculous deeds, popular Hellenic philosophy, and much else besides. But the popular catchword *syncretism*, like all catchwords, has done little to further historical understanding of the beginnings of Christianity, being true neither to classical Judaism, either in its native soil or in the Diaspora, nor to early Christianity. It is true that from the beginning ancient Israel and thereafter Judaism were always and variously exposed to foreign religious influences (from the earliest biblical text, the song of Deborah, dating from the twelfth century B.C., up unto the time of Jesus and Paul), but it was in such a context of attraction and repulsion that their religious identity was first established and furthermore strengthened, which is particularly true of the Hellenistic period in which foreign influences upon Judaism are said to have reached their climax. It is therefore not to be denied that Judaism had taken up numerous foreign influences, or perhaps one should say stimuli; but as the exilic and Persian periods show, these influences were either integrated or rejected.

In either case, such encounters effectively made Judaism more self-confident and influential, which is attested from the third century B.C. by the attraction of the synagogue for non-Jews and the great number of God-fearers who gathered in the Jewish houses of prayer. In fact, I would claim the same strong measure of self-identity for Qumran, the Pharisees, and the apocalyptic sects as I would for the translators of the Septuagint and Philo of Alexandria. In any case, the "syncretistic elements," which are overemphasized by such leading members of the *religionsgeschichtliche Schule* as H. Greßmann (e.g., in "Die Aufgaben der Wissenschaft des nachbiblischen Judentums," *Zeitschrift für die alttestamentliche Wissenschaft* 43, n.s. 2 [1925]: 1–32), have much more to do with pagan interest in Judaism than with Judaism itself. In comparison with their pagan surroundings, Judaism and early Christianity were not "syncretistic religions," unless one understands this notion to apply in a most general way to foreign influences of all kinds, in which case it becomes so general as to be empty.

2. From this thesis I would conclude first of all the following: It could be that whatever pagan influences have been suspected

in the origins of Christianity were mediated without exception by Judaism. For one can nowhere prove the *direct* influence of pagan cults or non-Jewish thought on early Christianity. What is described in the New Testament as Hellenistic could very well stem from Jewish sources that remained embedded in the religious *koinē*, the common religious language of the Hellenistic period. Only by participating in the religious language and imaginations of their day could they be attractive and have a certain effect — hence Judaism's rapid assimilation of the Greek language and its religious terms both in the Diaspora and even at home among its leading minds, as had already been the case with Aramaic during the Babylonian exile and the Persian period. Of course, at the time of Jesus and the apostles, Eretz Yisrael had stood under Greek influence for four hundred years, and one can therefore with complete justification designate the entirety of first- and second-century Judaism after Christ as Hellenistic — in other words, as stamped in various ways by the transmission of Hellenistic civilization and by conflict therewith.

If this is called syncretistic, then everything in Judaism of the Hellenistic era would have to be so called; consequently, the frequently used term *Hellenistic* is of as little use as the term *syncretistic* for making clear distinctions. Jerusalem, for example, the world-famous city of Jewish pilgrims, had its own unique brand of Hellenistic culture since the days of the Hasmoneans and Herod, namely, a special Jewish Hellenism that was different from that of Alexandria in that it was more strongly shaped by the Holy Land, the temple, and its cult. In any case, because so-called Palestinian Judaism, like the Jewish-Hellenistic Diaspora, formed anything but a unity, a clear and careful historical account of the matter stands in need of more precise characterizations than given by such catchwords as "syncretistic," "Hellenistic," or even "Palestinian." To cite another example, the Jews in Syria and Rome were more strongly under Palestinian influence than were, say, those in Alexandria and Egypt, who had a longer independent history going back to the sixth century B.C. To understand the matter better, we should therefore make distinctions among the spoken languages, such as Aramaic, Greek, and later Latin; likewise, for studies of Judaism and particularly of the early church, we should make geographical distinctions among Galilee, Jerusalem, Antioch, Alexandria, and Rome. In addition, we must also take note of differences regarding education and social conditions. For example, the Herodians and the priestly upper class in Jerusalem and the extremely wealthy family of Philo in Alexandria were much more Hellenized, which is to say, they received a better than average formal education. On the whole, Judaism in antiquity was much richer and more creative than is usually supposed.

3. Along with these Jewish foundations of the new, messianic movement, one must note that the great majority of the New Testament authors were Jewish Christians who for the most part either came from the Palestinian homeland or had some connection to it on account of their education and the groups to which they belonged. This last case applies above all to Paul, the earliest Christian author and scholarly trained Pharisee, who came from Tarsus to study in Jerusalem, but also to such figures as John Mark, the oldest Evangelist; it applies, furthermore, to the unknown (Syrian?) scribe and author of the Gospel of Matthew, the author of the Apocalypse of John, and the entire Johannine corpus. As far as I can see it, the author of the Fourth Gospel, who is identified with the "old one" (*ho presbyteros*) of the second and third letters of John, came from the priestly aristocracy of Jerusalem; as for Luke, the "beloved physician," he was probably a God-fearer or sympathizer before he became a Christian and later travel companion to Paul. His two-part work, unique among early Christian literature until Eusebius, demonstrates among all the non-Jewish authors of antiquity by far the best knowledge of Judaism both in the Diaspora and in the homeland.

One can furthermore presume that the unknown author of the Letter to the Hebrews was a rhetorically versed Hellenistic Jew who masterfully employed the Alexandrian art of allegorical and typological exegesis; similarly, that the author of Clement's first letter in Rome must have been familiar with the liturgy and scriptural tradition of the synagogue. For him, the Septuagint is the great collection of paradigms for correct church order. All in all, there remain few writings in the New Testament that one could in good conscience attribute to Gentile Christians. It is likewise reasonable to suspect that James, which is to some extent an anti-Pauline letter, was not written by a Gentile Christian, which would also seem to be true of the letter allegedly written by his brother, Jude. James, the brother of the Lord, is perhaps the real author, but the Letter of Jude is pseudonymous. The only remaining texts that could have been written by Gentile Christians are the very late pastoral letters, perhaps the somewhat earlier first letter of Peter (dating from around A.D. 100), and the considerably later second Petrine letter, which is in turn dependent upon Jude.

I know my view differs from that of many of my New Testament colleagues, but in my opinion they are too often inadequately acquainted with the Jewish sources to recognize the overwhelming Jewish substratum in the earliest Christian texts. As I see it, this is essentially an aftereffect of the old, latent anti-Jewish sentiment of German Idealism, which presumed that with the advent of Christianity and clear progress in the education of the human race the national religion of Judaism had lost its religious right to existence. Such regrettable lack of understanding regarding the Jewish cast of the majority of the New Testament texts is to be attributed perhaps above all to F. C. Baur and his students, who pointed scholarship in a one-sided direction with their precipitous evaluation of the difference between Palestinian, Jewish Christians and the universalistic Gentile Christianity inaugurated by Paul. At the same time, it is characteristic of early, apologetically motivated Jewish representations of Christianity, such as those of Heinrich Graetz, F. Perles, and I. Elbogen, that they readily accepted not only the Baur school's erroneously late datings of the New Testament writings but also its claims as to their historical unreliability and allegedly pagan origin so as to deny their value as serious sources. Anti-Judaism on the part of Christian scholars thus led to an anti-Christian response from Jewish scholars; given this circumstance, it is a credit to J. B. Lightfoot, Th. Zahn, Adolf von Harnack, and Adolf Schlatter that they established genuinely reliable markers for historical orientation. It was from them that both Kaufmann Kohler, the great advocate of Jewish reform, and Joseph Klausner, the brilliant Israeli historian, learned to treat the historical questions with much more care.

Inasmuch as the early history of the new, messianic movement of Christianity is also an important part of Jewish history, rigorous, destructive skepticism of this sort robs both Jewish and Christian historians of valuable information regarding their own respective histories. Unfortunately, since the Old Tübingen School, it has become common among some New Testament scholars to take pleasure in ruin, ravaging the sources and radically undermining their reliability. Once one has made a *tabula rasa* of the matter, however, one's own reconstructing fantasy can run wild. Thus, for the sake of historical reality and a shared history, Christian and Jewish scholars should make a common effort to guard against these destructive tendencies.

4. If this is the case, then the painful separation that took place between the synagogue and the new, enthusiastic-messianic movement was a long and complicated process and so cannot be clearly affixed to a definite and presumably early date. The term for this vexatious, end-of-time Jewish sect that went on to attain a place in history as *Christianoi* was in no way a self-description but probably was given to it by the pagan authorities in Antioch in connection with the troubles surrounding Caligula — for example, when the imperial paranoid wanted to erect a statue of himself in the temple in Jerusalem between A.D. 39 and 41. The newly discovered inscriptions from the trial of Gnaeus Piso, the governor of Syria and opponent of Germanicus, report that around 19 B.C. Roman soldiers in Antioch were divided between *Caesariani* and *Pisoniani;* this goes to show that this originally Latin word form of partisanship (*-iani*), which one also encounters in the term *Hērōdianoi*, was also common in the eastern, Greek-speaking part of the empire.

In the New Testament, the word *Christianoi* (=*Christiani*) occurs only three times, and of these, twice in the context of encounters with the Roman state. For Greek ears, the term should rather have been *Christaioi* or *Christenoi*. In fact, it was not until A.D. 114 that the Gentile martyr Ignatius used the word with frequency and distinguished, also for the first time, between Christianity (*Christianismos*) and Judaism (*Ioudaïsmos*), whereby it is interesting that Ignatius's expectation of martyrdom almost entirely overshadows any vision of the approaching end of the world. This goes to show that it was not until the first decades of the second century that the separation between mother and daughter was finally completed and the former Jewish eschatological movement had been transformed into a new, more universal religion.

At almost the same time Pliny writes to Trajan about his action regarding the *Christiani*, describing the matter as a *superstitio prava et immodica* ("a degenerate and extravagant superstition"); shortly thereafter Suetonius calls the Christian movement a *super-*

stitio nova et malefica ("a new and magical superstition"); but Tacitus still reports that this *exitiabilis superstitio* ("detestable superstition") began in Judea (which is to indicate its Jewish origins), was subsequently suppressed by Pilate, rose again, and from there made its way to Rome.

The Jewish description *noṣrîm/naṣrâyyâ/Nazoraioi,* on the other hand, is derived from the origin of Jesus of Nazareth and usually appears like the Greek *Nazarēnos* as an epithet for Jesus, in Hebrew: *Yešuaʿ ha-noṣrî* (cf. the analogous formation of *Essaios* and *Essēnoi*). It is furthermore noteworthy that during the trial of Paul, Tertullus, the rhetorical prosecutor from Jerusalem chosen by the high priest Ananias, speaks of the Jewish "sect of the Nazarenes" (Acts 24:5: *hē tōn Nazōraiōn hairesis;* cf. 24:15), whereas King Agrippa II uses the word *Christianos* (Acts 26:28). According to Luke, the high priest takes Paul to be a leader (*prōtostatēs*) of such an internal Jewish *hairesis*. Shortly thereafter Luke depicts Paul as a self-described one-time follower of the Pharisees, which is to name "the strictest *hairesis* of our religion" (Acts 26:5). In so doing Luke aptly states the facts regarding Christians and Pharisees: as he views it from the outside, Pharisees and *noṣrîm* are, though certainly different, nonetheless both Jewish *haireseis,* religious parties or sects. I find it interesting that on the Jewish side, the familiar Jewish name *Yešuaʿ,* the short form of *Yᵉhôšuaʿ,* does not disappear until the beginning of the second century, when it does so quite suddenly. Indeed, in his historical works Josephus still knows of twenty-two different "Jesuses." One also finds in Jerusalem many ossuary inscriptions with this name, but no rabbis would go on to bear the now cursed name.

5. It would follow, therefore, that the visible and often intense conflicts among various Jewish parties in the New Testament writings all testify to an internal-Jewish familial conflict — for instance, between the messianic "heresy" of the *noṣrîm* (the "Nazarene people"), the various other Jewish *haireseis* or groups in Judea such as the Pharisees, the Sadducees, the priestly aristocracy and the Herodians; and later the synagogue congregations of the Diaspora from Syria to Rome. In *My Brother Paul* (New York: Harper & Row, 1972, 115), Richard L. Rubinstein speaks of a "family dispute" and justifiably claims in view of Paul's harsh words in 1 Thessalonians 2:14–16 that "his harshness was not unlike that

of the members of the Community of the Scrolls." Family conflict is an old, biblical theme, which we already encounter in such
central Old Testament texts as those of Joseph and his brothers,
"Rebecca's children" (Alan Segal) and — most obviously — Cain
and Abel. Indeed, it is a fundamental human problem, and the thesis of conflict among siblings applies even to such texts as those
in the Gospel of John, where not only particular groups such as
the Scribes, Pharisees, and high priests are criticized, but even "the
Jews" themselves are sharply attacked.

But none of the New Testament authors could have known that
the messianic movement of the Nazarenes or *Christianoi* would
bring about a new religion alongside and in opposition to the Jews.
In fact, it is not in the New Testament but first in the apologists
of the second century, in the *Kerygma of Peter* and in Aristides,
that we encounter the notion of the Christians as a "third race"
or people alongside the Jews and Gentiles. Tertullian, for his part,
rejects the notion. At the outset, one was expecting anything but
the start of a new religion; rather, for Israel as for the world, one
was expecting the imminent arrival of the kingdom of God and the
parousia of Jesus of Nazareth, the crucified Messiah of Israel and
Son of God, who rose from the dead and was raised to the right
hand of God, that is, the prophesied Redeemer and Judge, both of
the people of God *and* of the nations of the world. In any case, the
arguments for this messianic and universalistic belief were taken
from the Jewish Bible.

The Nazarenes were thus separated from the rest of Israel by a
new, enthusiastic-eschatological faith that was nevertheless characteristically Jewish in detail. While the building itself was new, the
stones by which it was built were themselves Jewish. Even christology, the immediate source of difference, was basically Jewish in
character and in no way syncretistically pervaded by pagan influence. Likewise, the polemics of individual New Testament authors
from Paul to Luke and Matthew, and from there to John, were
no more intense than were those of the Essenes against "Ephraim"
and "Manasseh" (i.e., the Pharisees and the Sadducees), other Jewish groups. We must not forget that it already came to bloody
conflicts between Pharisees and Sadducees during the time of John
Hyrcanus and Alexander Jannai and then, once again, between
Zealots and peace advocates in the years before and after the outbreak of the Jewish war. The final motive of these battles was not

social but religious, and it consistently involved the controversial issue of *halakah* and eschatology (e.g., the rabbis later accused the pre-70 Zealots and Bar Kochba of wanting to force the eschaton). Was then the new proclamation that the Messiah had already come, the very one proclaimed as the Judge and Savior, whose speedy return was expected — phenomenologically understood — not also an expression of eschatological impatience or perhaps even of fanatic utopianism?

6. The question of anti-Judaism in the New Testament, which is frequently debated at the expense of the first Christian authors, has its place in view of the fateful, albeit unforeseeable, historical consequences (*Wirkungsgeschichte*) of some isolated texts, even if they were not "consequential" until centuries later. But at first the Jewish mother was clearly stronger than her unruly daughter. In view of the authors themselves, however, who awaited in their own lifetime the parousia of Jesus, the Messiah and Son of God, this accusation is anachronistic and remains so even for John. The young congregations lived in view of the approaching end and the coming of Christ, the Judge and Redeemer of the world. Standing under pressure from two sides — on the one hand, from the suspicious state authorities, on the other, from the stronger Jewish parent congregations, which were understandably enraged about the fanatic escapades of the new but still characteristically Jewish movement — they could not have foreseen the misuse of their polemical texts many centuries later. The family feud between the earliest Christian congregations and the synagogue — or more precisely, the various authorities of a more normative Judaism — was no more severe or injurious than were other internal Jewish conflicts that took place during the three hundred years of often intensive fighting from the Maccabean uprising up until the Bar Kochba revolt. But at the same time: family feuds are more painful and last longer than all others; and they happen to be this way precisely because one has so little distance from oneself, which is true of subsequent quarrels within the church up to this very day.

7. What was obvious about this conflict between a kind of growing, normative Judaism and the new messianic movement — I would almost say from the beginning on — was that it had clear contours and had to do with central religious concerns of Ju-

daism, that is, basic questions of Jewish theological belief, hope, and practice. In short, it had to do with the relation between messianic redemption and the traditional validity of the temple and the Torah. These last two, the temple and the Torah, which more or less comprised the heart of Jewish faith (at least in Palestine, where the conflict began) had already been threatened in connection with the radical attempt at Hellenic reform after 175 B.C., which called into question the identity of Israel as the people belonging to and chosen by God. From this time on, the Jews reacted allergically, even bitterly to every real and imaginary attack on these God-entrusted benefits and set themselves apart, at least in the mother country, even more sharply from the nations of the world. This was an understandable and even necessary reaction, but in the new messianic movement, in which Jesus was proclaimed as the crucified Messiah, the liberator from sin and death who was raised from the dead, it seemed that these most important benefits were once again being called into question, though for entirely different reasons than they had been two hundred years before.

At the time of Antiochus IV, the Jewish Hellenists had threatened the exclusivity of Jewish monotheism with their striving for secularization of the temple and integration among the nations of the world. But at this point monotheism was not the problem; rather, given the prospect of the imminent coming of the kingdom of God and the proclamation of the eschatological fulfillment of Old Testament prophecy, the significance of the temple and the Torah was being directly called into question. Faith (*'emûnâ*) and obedience were no longer directed primarily to the law, which was delivered to Israel on Sinai, but to a messianic person, a mediator, in whom the prayer of Isaiah (64:1) was to a certain extent fulfilled: "O that thou wouldst rend the heavens and come down." Indeed, God himself comes down to his people in the form of a human being, the seed of David promised by the prophets. Just as God the Father sends the *ḥokmâ*, the heavenly wisdom, according to the Jewish wisdom tradition of Ben Sira or Wisdom, he now sends to Israel the Son, who, as the servant of Isaiah 53, takes upon himself the sin of the world and redeems it vicariously through his death on the cursed tree: a message that could both fascinate and — even more — offend. This new heaven-storming messianic movement of the Nazarenes, which claimed for itself the eschatological gift of the prophetic Spirit, was also able to lay claim to some of the central doctrines of Israel's faith and did so, even in Eretz Yisrael itself, not without some measure of success.

Both the novelty and the danger of the enthusiastic-messianic *haireseis tōn Nazōraiōn* (Acts 24:5; cf. 24:14) lie in this central point of the person of Jesus — the Messiah, the *mᵉšiḥāʾ Yešuaʿ*, Christ Jesus — and the universal redemption that he put into effect. According to Luke, Tertullus characterizes the sect's ringleader, Paul, with understandable rage as "an instigator of rebellion among all Jews." In view of our earliest author, Paul, one could express the novelty of the matter in the catchy if somewhat exaggerated formula: "Messiah contra Torah." For it is no longer Moses and the law that mediates between God and humanity, but the messiah, Jesus, the bringer of the new covenant (cf. Jer. 31). Therefore, "Christ is the end of the law so that there may be righteousness for everyone who believes" (Rom. 10:4); accordingly, the Torah itself is no longer to be understood exclusively as the Jewish law but also as the law of God for all people, a law that is written even in the hearts of the pagans. It is the law, specifically, of the first commandment, of Deuteronomy 6:4 (to love God with all your heart), and of Leviticus 19:18 (to love your neighbor as yourself). According to Paul, the law serves primarily to demonstrate humanity's inability to obey God's holy will and gives, moreover, a "knowledge of sin" (Rom. 3:20) as the presupposition of grace.

While such a contradiction, or at least tension, between the Messiah and the Torah would undoubtedly have appeared absurd to orthodox Jews schooled in the law, it found a considerable echo among individual Jews in Jerusalem, as is evident from the stoning of Stephen, who "never ceases to speak words against this holy place and the law" (Acts 6:13). As a result, the Jewish Hellenists were expelled from the metropolis of Judea and became missionaries of the new messianic gospel in the synagogues of Syria. Moreover, thirty years later in A.D. 62, in an action that triggered protest among the Pharisees, Annas (Ananus) II, the son of the Annas of the passion story in John and brother-in-law of Caiaphas, ordered the execution by stoning of James, the brother of the Lord and by all accounts a law-abiding leader, and other Jewish Christians "as offenders of the law" (*hōs paranomēsantōn*, Josephus, *Ant.* 20 §200).

8. The expectation, founded on the manifold promises of the prophets, of a worldwide, eschatological conversion of the nations

to the one true God — namely, to the God of Israel and to the Savior he sent to his people — soon became central to the hopes of the new universalist, Jewish movement, especially through Paul and his friends. But how is this supposed to take place, if, as it says in the *Letter of Aristeas* (139), the Torah is what distinguished Israel from the nations, surrounding it "with impenetrable ramparts and iron walls," and if, according to *Abot* 1:1, these walls themselves needed the protection of an additional fence? In Galatians 3:23 even Paul is given to speaking of this insulating — but at the same time protecting — function of the Torah, though, to be sure, only until the sending of the Son into the world (i.e., until the "advent of faith"). Here we see a fundamental aporia in the prophetic faith of old Israel: the promise to the nations could become a full reality only if the barriers separating the Jewish people from "the converts to faith in the one God" were in some way overcome. This took place first and above all in the initial, eschatologically motivated Christian mission to the numerous God-fearers of the Diaspora synagogues in Syria.

In any case, in view of the future advent and the already effective reality of the kingdom of God, emphasis shifts from clear notions of Israel's exclusive existence and the earthly ethnicity of the Jews as a distinct political unit to a new, eschatological and universal consciousness. "For," to quote Paul, "in Christ you are all sons of God through faith.... There is neither Jew nor Greek, there is neither slave nor free, there is neither male nor female, for you are all one in Christ Jesus" (Gal. 3:26, 28). Or Philippians 3:20: "But our commonwealth (*politeuma*) is in heaven, and from there we await a Savior, the Lord Jesus Christ." Or Galatians 4:26: "But the Jerusalem above [in heaven] is free, and she is our mother"; moreover, according to Revelation 21 and 22, the holy city will come down out of heaven to a renewed creation and shelter the congregation of all the faithful, both Jews and Gentiles, as a place of God's eternal presence. On the other hand, emphasis upon the unity of exclusive, Torah-bound religion and political ethnicity gave classical Judaism its identity, an identity that proved to be stronger than all other religious groups of antiquity; of all the ancient religions only Judaism and Christianity survived. But here too an insurmountable difference with the new messianic, missions-oriented movement emerges, one that continues and is hotly debated even to this day: whereas in the state of Israel the national, religious legislation continues to work along the lines of the old theocratic ideal, a national Christian state, at least for to-day's Protestant, can only be a *contradictio in adjecto,* particularly in view of the revolutionary sentence of John 18:36 ("my kingdom is not of this world"). Its overcoming was effected by the Enlightenment (though for quite different reasons) and henceforth established in the American constitution's separation of church and state.

9. At the same time, the novelty of the movement provided its unheard-of offense, for — with its eschatological claims and the exemplary theological training of Paul, the former scribe and Pharisee — it was ultimately able to call into question the existence of Israel as a distinctive, elected people, that is, as a political-religious unity separated from the nations of the world. At least this was the accusation made against Paul, who holds to the election of all believers, be they from the Jews or the Gentiles; and even if he maintains that all of Israel is called by the grace of God to salvation, as in Romans 11:26 (which reminds one of Mishna, *Sanh.* 10.1), he also believes that at the end of history all nations will find their way back to God in the sign of the gospel, so that God's grace alone may triumph over all the powers of evil, sin, death, and the devil. Israel thereby becomes the great paradigm of grace, the "justification of the godless," as the one-time Pharisee and persecutor had himself experienced. Accordingly, the dogmatic part of Romans closes with the lapidary sentence: "For God has consigned all men to disobedience, *that he may have mercy upon them all*" (Rom. 11:32). "That he may have mercy upon them all," we may add, "in Christ," in the Messiah and Son of God. This is the last sentence of Paul's confession and the heart of the new message. Thereupon can only follow the hymn of praise: *soli Deo gloria,* as the only possible human answer to the grace of God. Could one imagine a more Jewish conclusion to a theological tract than this psalm-like gesture of praise: "O the depth of the riches and wisdom and knowledge of God!" which ends with the words "To him be glory forever! Amen" (Rom. 11:33–36)? The intense paraenesis that immediately follows is founded upon this experience of God's mercy, which should move one to answer God's grace, "to present one's body as a living sacrifice" and to "spiritual worship" (Rom. 12:1–2). Here we may speak of a new, eschatological and universal form of *kawwanah* or devotion.

Contrary to the hopes of apocalyptic utopianism, history obvi-

ously did not come to an end. More than three centuries later —
now well separated from its mother — the new and unexpectedly
victorious religion was burdened by the attainment of political power in the Roman Empire, a development that brought
with it an increasing sense of guilt, particularly in view of the
events of the second millennium. To this day, especially for those
Christians in Germany born before 1933, it bears the verdict of
self-righteousness and indifference with respect to the persecution
of the Jews. Unfortunately, it was not realized by many until it
was much too late that Hitler's regime was not only fervently
anti-Semitic but in its anti-Semitism also profoundly anti-Christian.

Early Christian Scripture as a Source
for Ancient Judaism

1. Appearing for the first time as a literary term at the beginning of third century in Tertullian and Clement of Alexandria, "the
New Testament" represents a collection of writings that grew entirely out of a Jewish milieu, both in the motherland as well as
in the Greek-speaking Diaspora; as such, it also represents a valuable source for the history and religion of Judaism at this time.
This holds true even if it can be accused of polemical distortions
in its representations, for instance, of the Scribes and Pharisees,
given that unbiased reporting in antiquity was all but nonexis-
tent. Furthermore, such an assessment of the New Testament as
a source for Judaism in antiquity would seem to be all the more
important given the paucity of sources and the fortuitousness of
their preservation. This state of affairs would seem to demand
that we earnestly assess, certainly with a critical eye, the value
of the sources we have in our possession rather than dismissing
them along the lines of a pseudo-critical skepticism. Moreover,
given that there are relatively few sources for classical Judaism
from the period of the Maccabees to Bar Kochba and from pre-
Constantinian Christianity in general, every substantial source text,
every bit of information, is bound to be of value; hence, along with
other sources, early Christian Scriptures constitute a special corpus
for Jewish history.

Of the other sources, surely the most important are those of
Josephus, whose dated historical reports in the *Bellum* and in the

Antiquitates first allow for an accurate placing of various names and phenomena; next Philo, the Jewish philosopher of religion, who could also be considered the father of the Platonizing theology of the early church; thereafter Jewish inscriptions and papyri, pagan information about Jesus, as well as the great number of apocryphal and pseudepigraphical texts, where in individual cases it is often difficult to distinguish between what is Jewish and what is Christian; then early Talmudic literature (i.e., the Mishna, Tosefta, the tannaitic Midrashim and the Baraitot of the two Talmuds and the later Midrashim); and finally, last but not least, the texts of Qumran, which in my judgment represent the most important collection of sources to be discovered in the twentieth century. These Qumran texts likewise point to an independent, eschatological movement that, on account of its particular interpretation of the Torah and the prophets, separated itself from the rest of the nation, which it rejected as the *massa perditionis*. As it is written in the decisive halachic, eschatological sentence of 4QMMT: "We have separated ourselves from the mass of the people." Given such a diverse collection of Jewish text forms — which reveal a spiritual wealth and creativity without parallel in the religious world of antiquity — the question naturally arises whether one should not also be able to cite the texts of early Christianity, however eccentric, as Jewish sources, since they too enrich our knowledge of classical Judaism to a considerable degree.

Like the corpus of the Septuagint, these early Christian texts can be divided into reportive, instructional, and apocalyptic writings; but even the smaller narrative, paraenetical and liturgical forms — miracle narratives, parables, proverbs, passion and martyr reports, and religious sayings in the form of midrash, legends, hymns, articles of faith, prayers, blessings, visions — all correspond to those of Jewish literature, be they in Hebrew, Aramaic, or Greek. Moreover, they correspond to Jewish sources to a much greater degree than to those characteristically rhetorical and poetic forms that are common in pagan Greek literature. In respect to its form, typical Jewish Hellenistic literature, strictly understood, follows Greek examples to a greater degree than does the New Testament. It is no coincidence that until the Nazarene Gnostic Valentinus, we find no religious hymns with a quantifiable, typical Greek meter in all of early Christian literature, but we do find, often enough, a Semitic *parallelismus membrorum;* in regard to its own new song, the early

church adopted from the Septuagint a distinctly Jewish understanding of the concept of the psalm, whereby its classical meaning,
"string music," was changed to that of a hymnic song. Early Christian literature is as little a matter of philosophical literature as it is
of epic or drama, and if they occur at all, quotations from classical poets are rare exceptions; accordingly, they are expressions not
of higher literary education but of simple, indigenous proverbs. In
contrast to the Christian texts, one finds them relatively often in
Jewish Hellenistic literature, for example, as later quoted by such
educated Christian authors as Clement of Alexandria, Eusebius,
and Pseudo-Justin. But until Clement of Alexandria, none of the
early Christian authors possessed a Greek learning comparable to
that of Philo. As it happens, the first signs of deeper literary eru-
dition among the Christians, with the exception of Luke, are to be
found in such early Gnostics as Basilides, Carpocrates, and Valentinus. This would imply, however, that a history of classical Jewish
literature would have to include that of early Christianity, even if
the latter went on to become independent and go its own way.

Jewish scholarship could here run a fruitful and stimulating
competition with present scholarship of the New Testament, which
at times can be somewhat sterile; and for this we Christian
theologians would have to be thankful. For just as Jewish parallels help to illumine New Testament texts and render their
historical-philological context more understandable, so can these
early Christian texts, now better understood, in turn shed a degree
of light on the Jewish sources. The Pharisees, for example, appear
ninety-nine more times in the New Testament than in Josephus and
the Talmudic literature combined; and even if the Gospels and the
Acts portray them mostly in a polemical light, these Jewish Christian reports round out and lend more credibility to the picture one
receives from the other two Jewish sources. Furthermore, even if
the latest canonical Gospels of Matthew and John tend to overemphasize the authority of the Pharisees, the New Testament texts
in their entirety only confirm what continues to be illegitimately
disputed, namely, their leading role in the spiritual and religious
matters of the Jewish people, which they already had prior to the
catastrophe of A.D. 70. According to Mark and Luke but in contrast to the later Matthew, the same is true of the scribes, who
are to be distinguished from the Pharisees. While the Pharisees and
scribes appear in Galilee, the priestly aristocratic Sadducees (about

whom Luke seems to have been most informed given his account in the Acts) are found only in Jerusalem. In spite of the findings of Qumran, the fact that the Essenes do not appear in the New Testament should serve as a warning that one not overemphasize their significance. Unlike the Pharisees, they were not involved with the teaching of the law to the common people but were rather the true separatists. Jewish-Christian scholarship is therefore not helped if one overcomes an outdated pan-Gnosticism only to assert a pan-Essenism in its place.

2. We are already thick among details, and though the whole matter warrants an independent monograph, I can at present only pick out a few more or less arbitrary examples. Surprisingly enough, all four Gospels narrate only events from Eretz Yisrael, that is, they restrict themselves to Jesus' sojourn in Galilee and his journey from there to Jerusalem. As it happens, the geographical information they provide is more reliable than is assumed by contemporary scholarship, which is, unfortunately, geographically uninformed. The paucity of references to non-Jewish, pagan territories in Palestine should also serve to confirm this picture. Of many possible examples, take the following: John 4:5 notes "a Samaritan city named Sychar"; this, as it happens, is the first historical record of the Samaritans' largest settlement following the destruction of their old capital, Shechem, at the hands of John Hyrcanus. In the later Samaritan sources the place appears as Askar (*'śśkwr*), today as Askor, and in the Mishna and later Talmudic sources as Sokher; in any case, located approximately one to two kilometers from the ruins of Shechem. All in all, the Fourth Gospel provides a relatively large amount of detailed geographical and historical information.

Josephus's report concerning the life and death of John the Baptist cannot be understood apart from the baptismal accounts of the Synoptics, especially of Q. Here, in addition to the three or four "religious parties" described by Josephus, an independent eschatological and ascetic penitence movement comes into view. On the one hand, it has a certain parallel in the unusual, autobiographical story of Josephus concerning the hermit Bannus; on the other, is clearly connected with late Jewish baptismal sects of the kind attested to by such church fathers as Epiphanius. Interestingly enough, the Pseudo-Clementine novel sees the Baptist in connection with such dark Samaritan religious figures as Dositheos and Simon Magus. But given the notorious lack of sources, we can do little more than discern from a distance certain traces of religious pluralism and sectarianism.

3. There is broad consensus that Jesus arises out of the Jewish baptismal movement of his day; in fact, nineteenth-century Jewish historians had already discounted the old Jewish polemic, which was picked up by Celsus and furthered by the *Toledot Yešû*, that Jesus was the illegitimate son of a Roman soldier named Panthera. The end of the nineteenth century was witness to a new round of absurd claims, for example, the typical social-Darwinistic detritus of the previous century circulated by such figures as Houston Stewart Chamberlain, the son-in-law of Richard Wagner, to the effect that Jesus was not of Jewish but Aryan descent. (*Die Grundlagen des neunzehnten Jahrhunderts* [Munich: F. Bruckmann, 1938]; cf. P. Haupt, "The Aryan Ancestry of Jesus," *The Open Court* 23 [1909]: 193–209). It is a disgrace that such famous German Christian theologians as W. Grundmann and E. Hirsch furthered such anti-Semitic nonsense. After all, on the first page of their 1922 commentary H. L. Strack and P. Billerbeck had already dismissed such claims as "completely empty." This means that Jesus had already been recovered into the context of Judaism at the beginning of the twentieth century; indeed, Julius Wellhausen's lapidary statement that "Jesus was not a Christian, but a Jew" is generally undisputed. Thus, in *Das Urchristentum im Rahmen der antiken Religionen* (Zürich: Artemis-Verlag, 1949; ET, *Primitive Christianity in Its Contemporary Setting*, trans. R. H. Fuller, London: Thames & Hudson, 1956), Bultmann presents "the proclamation of Jesus" not in the chapter concerning the beginning of Christianity but in the chapter on Judaism. Likewise, his 1948 theology begins with the lapidary statement: "The proclamation of Jesus belongs to the presuppositions of a theology of the New Testament, not to a theology of the New Testament proper." In other words, for Bultmann, Jesus belonged entirely within the context of Judaism, a position that earned him the criticism of his colleagues but to which he held throughout, referring, among other things, to the fact that "modern Jewish theologians claim Jesus in their own right."

As far as I'm concerned, this is really a pseudo-dispute, for Jesus belongs to both Jews and Christians. And though they dissented relatively quickly precisely in regard to his person and soteriological significance, it would seem feasible that his person could once again lead both closer together, even if the dissent stems from questions regarding his claim and the relevance of his person. Be that as it may, it is beyond doubt that Christianity began *in nuce* with the public appearance of Jesus or, for that matter, the calling of the disciples; and the whole dispute goes but to show that Christianity is entirely rooted in Judaism — I would argue that it continued to be so for nearly a century.

What is disputed today, particularly among Jewish scholars, is to what kind of Judaism Jesus belongs. Following Christian authors since the eighteenth century, Graetz and Kohler placed him in proximity to the Essenes; Klausner depicted him as a quietistic Pharisee; Geza Vermes, as a Galilean Ḥasid and miracle worker; and R. Eisler, among others, as a Zealot. Other possibilities include the picture of a rabbi, a prophet, a magician, and, of course, according to the four Gospels — though many New Testament scholars wish to deny it — the proclaimed Messiah; or — according to the latest fashion — a rustic, Jewish Socrates with a touch of cynicism. Interestingly enough, this kaleidoscopic picture of Jesus mirrors in analogous fashion the entire religious inventory of Palestinian Judaism, as well as the creative fantasy of both Christian and Jewish scholars.

The Gospels, particularly the Synoptics, thus introduce one into the middle of Jewish history, into its very heart, the history of first-century Jewish religion. As such, next to the *Vita* of Josephus, the Gospels are the oldest datable sources for the religious and social customs of Galileans at that time, as are in particular the parables of Jesus for the given social environment with its tenants, farmers, landholders, slaves, tax collectors, and lenders. The double "trial" of Jesus before the high priest and the Roman prefect is, furthermore, the most extensive source for proceedings in a capital case against a simple provincial, not only in Judea but in the whole Roman Empire before the acts of the martyrs. In reality it was little more than an ostentatious apprehension and execution of an individual for the sake of upholding peace and public order, an act of *coercitio* by the civil authorities. As is often noted, there are parallels here between the proceedings of the Jerusalem authorities and those of the procurator Albinus against Jesus son of Ananias,

the mischievous prophet, shortly before the outbreak of the Jewish
war (Josephus *War* 6 §300). The proceedings against Jesus demonstrate how sensitively the prefect and the priestly aristocrats of the
Annas clan reacted to suspicions of messianic claims; and in this
regard, particularly in view of new parallels from Qumran, there
can be no doubt that Jesus made claims to being the final Prophet,
which is to say, the *māšiaḥ* anointed by the Spirit (Isa. 61:1). The
prosecution politically distorted this claim to suggest that this men-
dicant, Galilean preacher and prophetically "anointed" individual
posed a danger not only to peace and public order but even to
Rome itself. One begins to understand the matter from the title
given to Jesus on the cross, "King of the Jews." The title not only
made public the *causa poenae* but also served as a sign of intimida-
tion and mockery of the Jewish people. The construction is clearly
not Christian in origin, but while the "King of the Jews" appears
nowhere as a christological title, it appears often enough among
Jewish rebels. Thus, before Pilate, the original charge against Jesus
as the prophetic Messiah becomes a charge against "the King of
the Jews."

Even John, the latest of the Gospels, which takes a notable liberty in the arrangement of history and tradition, proves to be the
source of many valuable historical insights, for example, regarding
Pilate's dealings with the high-priestly figure Annas and his son-
in-law Caiaphas. The same is true in regard to Jewish pilgrimage
festivals. For example, it is first in John that we find the Greek
equivalent for the Ḥanukkah festival, *ta engkainia* (John 10:22),
which is celebrated in the winter approximately two months after
the festival of booths. Second Maccabees 1:9 refers to it as the "festival of booths in the month of Chislev," and Josephus (*Ant.* 12
§325) refers to it as a "festival of lights" (*phōta*). These are but a
few of many examples of the Fourth Gospel's deep roots in Jewish
tradition, the one Gospel, as it happens, that to the outside readily
appeared anti-Jewish.

In John 4:22 we read the words of Jesus to the Samaritan
woman: "You worship what you do not know; we worship what
we know, for salvation is from the Jews." For critical exegetes like
Bultmann and those of his school this statement was so offensive
that they denied its authorship to the Evangelist and marked it
as a late addition of an "ecclesiastical redactor." In reality, Jesus'
statement says the same thing as John 10:34, namely, that God's

revelation is directed to Israel. As witnessed to by Scripture, the *logos tou theou* became man in Israel, specifically, in Jesus of Nazareth, the Son of God and Messiah sent by the Father into the world. Moreover, in John, Pilate addresses Jesus not only as a Jew but as the King of the Jews, a title that is foreign to New Testament christology, but which Jesus himself does not deny. As such, I would have to argue that the Fourth Gospel is unintelligible apart from its Jewish background, which is attested to not only by the numerous allusions to the Old Testament but also by many connections to Jewish interpretation in the Midrashim. As Schlatter had already pointed out, there are also significant linguistic similarities to the tannaitic Midrashim and above all to the Mekhilta of Exodus. In short, the author of the Fourth Gospel thought Hebraically; and as H. Gese has convincingly demonstrated in "The Prologue to John's Gospel," (in his *Essays on Biblical Theology* [Minneapolis: Augsburg, 1981], 167–222]), the prologue of the Gospel is itself Hebraic in structure: in view of the dualism between light and darkness, the understanding of *'mt / alētheia,* and the doctrine of predestination, the author of the Fourth Gospel stands not only in proximity to Qumran but is also clearly familiar with the Tanakh and the Jewish purity *halacha.* As for the key text in John 2:6, with the six huge, stone jars "for the Jewish rites of purification," each holding twenty or thirty gallons, I might point out R. Deines's careful study, which is founded upon Jewish archaeological findings (*Jüdischer Steingefäße und pharisäische Frömmigkeit,* WUNT 2.52 [Tübingen: J. C. B. Mohr (Paul Siebeck), 1993]).

4. It took a considerably longer time before Paul, the earliest author of the New Testament, was rediscovered as a Jew, even though he, more than any of the other early Christian authors, emphasizes his Jewish roots, his descent from Abraham — specifically, his descent from the tribe of Benjamin — and his ties to the Hebrew- and Aramaic-speaking Jewry of his mother country. I have already pointed out his affiliation with the religious party of the Pharisees, which he himself accentuates and which Luke emphasizes to an even greater degree. In this regard I might point out the recent Heidelberg dissertation of Stefan Meissner, significantly titled *Die Heimholung des Ketzers: Studien zur jüdischen Auseinandersetzung mit Paulus* (WUNT 2.87 [Tübingen: J. C. B. Mohr (Paul Siebeck), 1996]). Against considerably earlier attempts

to "recover" Jesus within a Jewish context, he finds a paradigm change to have taken place with regard to Paul only in the last few decades and concludes: "This development, which is not entirely dissimilar to previous attempts to reconsider the person of Jesus within Judaism, is characterized above all by the fact that Jewish interpreters today lend more value than previously to the Jewish roots of Paul's theology." In other words, it was previously common "to separate the apostle from Judaism" by claiming that he was "influenced by pagan ideas," as did Samuel Hirsch, Graetz, Kohler, and even, at an early stage, Leo Baeck. In the last two figures a certain influence from the history of religions school is unmistakable, which assumed the apostle to be under the massive influence of Hellenistic syncretism and — above all in his christology — a pre-Christian gnosis; this remains true for Bultmann and his school as well.

Jewish authors, by contrast, compared Paul with the rabbinic sources, where they discovered some parallels but more often insurmountable differences. Since then our knowledge of the sources has increased considerably, due not only to the discoveries of Qumran and the Pseudepigrapha, but also to the work of Gershom Scholem, I. Grünwald, and P. Schäfer, in particular, as regards the light they have shed upon Jewish mysticism. Even C. G. Montefiore, "the first Jewish scholar of the New Testament," who was also the first to realize "that the New Testament represents an important part of the Jewish literature of antiquity," saw in Paul a degenerate form of Diaspora Judaism at work — one broken up, that is, by pagan influences. It remains to be said that he was influenced by such figures as W. Bousset, R. Reitzenstein, and A. Loisy and measured the apostle with an anachronistic, rabbinical yardstick. But as a radical originator of reform, Montefiore also found some positive trains of thought in Paul — among others, that in spite of all established differences, he was "the first to preach and practice a consistent universalism." Furthermore, though he rejected Paul's critique of the law, he found it not without certain positive aspects. It was the Pauline ethic and praise of *agape* ("love"), however, that claimed the attention of this Jewish intellectual, but through the glass of his interpretation, which was ahead of his time, these very themes became the subject of vehement critique among his fellow Jews.

On the basis of "thorough research over many decades," Klausner "came to the conclusion that there was nothing in the teachings of Paul — not even in the majority of mystical passages — that could not be derived from Judaism in its original form," which goes to say that he denies any immediate influence "from Greek philosophical literature or the mystery religions." Nevertheless, as a self-conscious Zionist who attached little value to the Diaspora, he ultimately comes to the conclusion regarding Paul, a Jew of the Diaspora, that "most of the elements in his teaching which derive from Judaism" received "a non-Jewish coloring" due to the "influence of the Jewish-Hellenistic and pagan atmosphere" in which he lived. Hence, in the end, he "led the Jews who believed in Jesus out of Judaism and . . . after some time, imperceptibly, into a compromising, half-pagan sect" that "was a combination of Judaism and paganism." To be sure, this was not Paul's intention, but since Christianity was for him supposed to be a kind of new, reformed Judaism (so Klausner) and since he separated the Jews and Gentiles who believed in Jesus from the older Jewish communities, "a fundamentally new religion inevitably arose . . . in which only a part of Judaism remains."

In spite of his one-sided Zionist tendencies, Klausner was in my opinion the first among Jewish interpreters of Paul to have some essential insights, even if he failed to recognize adequately the apostle's eschatological motivation, even if he misunderstood the Pauline doctrine of grace, for which he never really had much interest, and even if he overemphasizes the difference between the Diaspora and the homeland. No Jewish scholar before him had worked out to such a degree the numerous Jewish parallels to Paul's letters; it is interesting that he accepted the thesis of liberal Protestant scholarship that Paul was the actual founder of Christianity. In the well-known, nearly confessional, messianic outlook at the end of his work, which I take to be more important than his book on Jesus, he claims that "a purified Judaism will know how to appreciate Paul's great merit." In a purified form, Paul is for him "a forerunner of the King Messiah."

H. J. Schoeps's 1958 book on Paul represented a truly new approach to Jewish interpretations of Paul. In contrast to older Jewish scholarship (with the exception of Klausner) he rejects interpretations of the apostle that read him in light of syncretistic pagan Hellenism as well those which see him one-sidedly as a product of Hellenistic Judaism. Importantly, he makes the insightful observation that Paul is stamped by a Palestinian Jewish apocalypticism that does not stand in opposition to the rabbinical tradition. What is new and decisive in Paul is that the new age has already broken in, that the Messiah has already come; as such, according to the title of the second paragraph of the book, Paul is a "thinker in a post-messianic situation." Following older Jewish scholars, Schoeps explains Paul's understanding of the end of the law in connection with the advent of the messianic age; moreover, in regard to the human fall into sin, he refers not only to the "evil urge" and the fourth book of Ezra but also to texts from Qumran. For Schoeps, Paul's understanding of the economy of salvation and his crowning eschatological universalism, in which he "views the evangelization of the Gentiles as a kind of acceleration of the eschaton," are likewise rooted entirely within the scope of Jewish tradition. On the other hand, in Paul's christology and its themes of divine sonship, preexistence, incarnation, and a mysticism of Christ's body, he finds certain pagan influences at work. But here, I would argue, Schoeps failed to immerse himself deeply enough in contemporary, Jewish religious history. This point has been developed further by younger Jewish scholars, who have pointed out Pauline parallels in Jewish mysticism. Samuel Sandmel, for example, who was only two years younger than Schoeps, placed Paul completely within the context of Hellenistic Judaism and recognized, contrary to the traditional view, that Paul posed no threat to the purity of Jewish monotheism, since it is ultimately God who works through Christ and since the formula "to be in Christ" signifies the working of the Holy Spirit. At the same time, as a convinced reformer, he realized the present-day significance of the apostle as a critic of enshrined religious institutions and for this reason preferred him to the Gospels.

5. Oddly enough, the rediscovery of the apostle as a Jewish thinker occurred where Jewish intellectual protest was initially the strongest: at the center of his theology, that is, the turn in his life and the christology intimately connected therewith. Thus Paul is brought within the context of Jewish mysticism, in spite of the fact that postwar, German New Testament scholarship, going against Adolf Deissmann and Albert Schweitzer, had rejected such notions. Ultimately it is a question of definition and one's own religious point of view, for if mysticism is defined as a form of self-redemption from the depths of one's own or even the di-

vine self, then the concept is off mark; but if it is employed as a phenomenological concept to describe religious experience, then it finds some legitimation. For too long scholars have defined mysticism along neo-Platonic lines and, consequently overlooked Jewish mysticism proper and its specific roots in prophecy and apocalypticism. The fact that Paul was at the same time a penetrating theological thinker makes no difference: for thought and ecstatic mystical experience are as little exclusive as are thought and the reception of divine revelation. It was none other than Scholem who called Paul the "most exceptional example of a revolutionary Jewish mystic," in whose case the interpretation of his "mystical experience leads . . . to a complete breaking of the bounds of traditional authority." Indeed, as he further contends: "Paul represents in all sharpness the paradigmatic collision of the mystic with the religious authorities."

Jewish scholarship has long since recognized connections to a divine mediator within the Pauline and Johannine christologies, and though they were devalued as marginal, the same remains true of such Jewish Hellenistic and apocalyptic parallels as the Jewish personification of wisdom, her mission in the world, and the apocalyptic, preexistent Son of Man. Alan Segal has made significant efforts towards clarifying this matter in his exceptional study, *Paul the Convert* (New Haven, Conn.: Yale University Press, 1990), in which he sees the influence of ideas from *Hekhalot* mysticism and apocalypticism already at play in Paul's vision of Christ on the road to Damascus, ideas that would come to play a significant role in the formation of the Pauline christology. One already finds the sending of Wisdom to Zion in Sirach and to pious men and prophets in Wisdom, but the texts from Qumran, which precede the parables of the Ethiopian Enoch (whose dating still remains disputed), first give us pre-Christian parallels to Merkaba mysticism. It is noteworthy, for example, that in 11QMelch Melchizedek is presented according to the representation of Michael: Melchizedek as the "heavenly redeemer," to whom is attributed a more or less divine dignity, as in the citation of Isaiah 52:7: *mālaḵ ʾelōhāyiḵ* ("thy God has become king") and in similar fashion to the preexistent Christ in the christological hymn of Philippians 2:6–11. Ultimately, one line extends from the preexistent Son of Man / Messiah of the parables, who is connected with the figure of Enoch in texts like Daniel 7, Psalm 110, and Isaiah 52:13, to the Metatron and the "little Yahweh" of the late 3 Enoch and Merkaba mysticism.

In the so-called Prayer of Joseph (Origen, *Commentary on John* 2.31) Jacob/Israel appears as the embodiment of the highest angel, and Philo can call the divine Logos the archangel, the Son of God, and even a *deuteros theos*, "second God." This goes to show that even the high christology that one finds in an advanced form in Paul and completed in John is not without many Jewish analogies both in Palestinian Judaism and in the Diaspora. The only question that remains is whether and to what extent they correspond to the distinctive, early Christian understanding of the relationship between the Father and the Son. Concerning the incarnation, crucifixion, and exaltation of Christ, it is no coincidence that early Christian thought was led to a trinitarian concept of God, and one sees the first signs of this already in Paul's and Hebrews' fundamental distinction between the preexistent, glorified Christ and the angels beneath him.

Thus, on the whole, while they are founded upon a Jewish background and built, as it were, with Jewish stones, it seems to me that the Pauline and Johannine christologies are of a distinctly new character that exceeds historical derivation and is grounded in an original religious experience and reflection. For my part, as a Christian theologian, I do not hesitate to speak here of a direct revelation: the sending of the eschatological redeemer to the world (or more precisely, to the people of God), his messianic ministry vis-à-vis Israel, his vicarious atonement on the cross, his resurrection and ascension to the right hand of God, and the expectation of his coming as Judge and Redeemer all form a unity that leans entirely upon Old Testament and Jewish conceptions and yet presents a message so new as to evoke offense. The identification of the risen Christ with the Kyrios of the Septuagint is prefigured on the one hand by the appellation of the risen Christ in the Palestinian community as *maran* ("our Lord," 1 Cor. 16:22) and on the other hand by the elevation of *'adōnî* (="my Lord," i.e., the resurrected Son, Jesus of Nazareth) to the right hand of *'adōnay* (the "Lord," the Father, i.e., according to Ps. 110:1, God himself), with whom he sits on the Merkaba throne. Just as the third verse would seem to speak of his original preexistence, it seems to me that the entire psalm refers to him, the resurrected one, practically from the beginning. The fact that the title *Lord* is applied to Jesus and that texts like Joel 2:32 (Heb. 3:5), which originally referred to God himself, came to be interpreted in reference to the glorified Lord Jesus, should be seen in connection with such Old Testament texts as Exodus 23:20–21, which refer to the *mal'āḵ 'ᵃḏōnay* with the divine name (i.e., the tetragrammaton: *kî šᵉmî bᵉqirbô;* LXX: *to gar onoma mou estin ep' autō,* "for my name is on him"). This development seems to have taken place relatively quickly after Easter in Eretz Yisrael; following the paschal death of Christ, something like a spiritual explosion must have taken place among the disciples, one that spread out like shock waves.

Not least to be noted is the fact that Paul's doctrine of justification, which represents nothing less than the centerpiece of his message, rests entirely upon a Jewish foundation. The fact that God justifies the unrighteous who trust completely in his will and salvation is a central notion of the Gospels, whose onset we find in the texts of Qumran, in some Psalms, in Deutero-Isaiah, and elsewhere in the Old Testament. In my opinion, the characteristically Pauline notion of living "in Christ" (*en christō*) or "in the Lord" (*en kyriō*), which today is once again being interpreted mystically, was originally formed as a parallel construction to *en nomō* ("in the law") or, as the case may be, *hypo nomon* ("under the law") and circumscribes a belonging to Christ and the realm of salvation he prepared. The fact that the law brings about a knowledge of sin (Rom. 3:20) does not express an antinomianism but God's holiness; hence, in spite of its power to bring about the death of the sinful person, "the law is holy, and the commandment is holy and just and good" (Rom. 7:12). Knowledge of the holy inexorability of the Torah, which nevertheless concentrates on the first commandment and the double commandment of love, is a necessary and salutary preparation for the knowledge of God's universal redemption of humanity through the death of his Son. At no point does Paul step out of Jewish categories, even when his soteriological reflections may sound unusual, if not offensive; moreover, his christology and soteriology have nothing to do with Oriental vegetation mythology, for example, or with the yearly death and rejuvenation of Osiris or Adonis.

Paul's letters thus bear witness to the revolutionary effects of the religious worldview of a messianic Jewish movement in *statu nascendi,* paradigmatically represented in the theology of an exceptional Jewish thinker and scribe. The extent to which he remained a Jew is clear from Romans 9–11, which culminate in 11:26: "And so all Israel will be saved," a statement that is generally recognized to be closely related to Mishna, *Sanh.* 10.1: "All of Israel has a share in the coming world." Surely a prominent messianic and mystical thinker like Paul should not be without a place in accounts of Israel's religious history up to the time of the Mishna and the Talmud.

6. If the letters of Paul represent an original, albeit unconventional source for the history of Jewish religious thought of the first century, then in a like but different manner this should also be true of Luke's Acts of the Apostles, which includes, among other things, a considerable amount of political and social history. As with Bultmann and before him the Tübingen school of Baur, some Jewish scholars have made the sure mistake of overlooking its value as a historical source. According to Baeck, it is, as with the Third Gospel, more like "historical *belles-lettres* than actual history," and Sandmel has a similarly low opinion of its worth as a source, dating its authorship at around 115 and finding it to possess no "weighty, reliable information on Paul." Unjustly so. For Luke not only bears many similarities to Josephus as a contemporary interested in Judaism (with whom, one might add, Sandmel is insufficiently acquainted), but after Josephus and Philo's two historical writings, the Acts represents the most important source for the history of Judaism between Herod and A.D. 70. This is true not only for an understanding of the political powers in Judea up to the time of the procurators Felix and Festus (and thereafter King Agrippa II and his sister) but also for an understanding of the Hellenistic milieu in Jerusalem itself, the world-renowned pilgrim's city, with its countless visitors from Hellenistic synagogues of the Diaspora, among whom was a small group of Greek-speaking, messianic Jews, the so-called Hellenists of Acts 6, who stirred up trouble under the leadership of a figure named Stephen. It is important to note that the original Christian missions in the Diaspora of the Roman Empire grew precisely out of this milieu.

We are indebted to Luke, among other things, for the oldest depictions of worship in the synagogue (Luke 4; Acts 13); the speeches in Acts are to a certain extent like summary synagogue speeches with salvific, messianic content. We find, furthermore, completely accurate characterizations of the Jewish parties of the

Pharisees and Sadducees. For example, Luke depicts Gamaliel as the leading Pharisee and teacher of Paul, while Josephus depicts his son, Simon, as the moderate head of the Pharisees at the outbreak of the war in A.D. 66. There is, furthermore, an ossuary inscription from Jerusalem that likely bears reference to John (*Iōannēs*), the puzzling figure of the high priest's family mentioned in Acts 4:6; it also refers to a figure named Yohanna, daughter of the priest Yohanan and granddaughter of the high priest Theophilos, who was himself a son of the New Testament figure Annas, the high priest between 6 and 15. That this Annas was the father-in-law of Caiaphas, the high priest from 18 to 36, we learn only from John 18:13. Between 6 and 41 and especially during the time of Pilate (26–36), the clan of Annas apparently had Jerusalem well under its control, which would not seem to have changed until 41 and the reign of Agrippa I. So it is no historical error on the part of Luke when he names Annas and Caiaphas as high priests in Luke 3:2 (cf. Acts 4:6). It is also possible that the synagogue of the *Libertinoi* (the freed Jews who came from Rome [Acts 6:9]), is the same building that, according to a famous inscription, was founded by Theodotos, son of Vettenus, and also served as a hostel for pilgrims. The last member of the seven in Acts 6:5, Nicolaus, a proselyte from Antioch, likewise has his parallels in a more recent inscription that mentions a figure named Ariston, a proselyte from Apamea (who, as it happens, is also mentioned in the Mishna, *Halla* 4.11). One could go on to list many more historical details. As it is, they do not fit in with the popular picture of Luke as a kind of pious, ahistorical novelist nor, for that matter, with the fashionable picture of the later, apocryphal Acts of the Apostles, partially based on Luke's account, written during the second half of the second century.

Luke's reference to large, influential groups of God-fearers or sympathizers, who were mostly women and who gathered in the cities around core Jewish communities, is of foundational importance for understanding both the Pauline mission and the structure of the Diaspora communities in the big cities at that time. The significance of these groups even at a much later date has been confirmed by a large inscription of Aphrodisias, which corrects the absurd hypothesis of A. T. Kraabel that there were no God-fearers and sets the matter once again in the right light. Here as well, Luke and Josephus touch upon a common basis. Josephus, for example, reports numerous noble women as being sympathizers of the large Jewish community in Damascus and also testifies of the attraction of the Jewish communities for non-Jews in Antioch. Luke gives a similar report of Pisidian Antioch and other cities. He also depicts Paul as appearing with a certain regularity in urban synagogues along his missionary route, where he addresses not only the Jews but also the sympathizers, who are the very ones to give him the most positive response; after a short time, this leads to his expulsion and the independent establishment of a messianic community. This is presumably the pattern according to which the communities founded by Paul were established. That is to say, the Gentile Christians that appear in Paul's letters, for example, Titus, whom he brought along to the apostolic council in Jerusalem, and Luke himself, were first and foremost such sympathizers.

This alone explains how Paul's missionary sermons and then his letters, with their demanding scribal argumentation, could have been understood. For the average devotees of indigenous pagan cults, say, of Zeus, Dionysus, Serapis, the Dea Syria, or Isis, his message would at first have been incomprehensible. The word *Christos,* which in Greek did not even denote a person, literally meant someone "smeared" or "anointed" and was therefore, due to a simple itacism, misunderstood as the slave name *Chrestos.* In other words, a good part of Paul's addressees were from the beginning sympathizers, pagans who must have been at least somewhat familiar with the Septuagint, which was read aloud in the synagogue on the sabbath. Like the sermons in Acts, his letters are therefore an important source for understanding synagogue interpretations of Holy Scripture in the Diaspora, particularly given the fact that so few synagogue sermons have survived.

Next to the passion narratives, the juridical process against Paul, first in Jerusalem and then in Caesarea, is without a doubt the most extensive portrayal of a provincial Roman trial that we possess. In the case of Paul, the trial was not against a provincial like Jesus, but against a Roman citizen who was skilled in rhetoric, knew how to defend himself, and in the end appealed to the emperor. In my opinion, the vivid portrayal of these events is to be traced back to the eyewitness of Luke, for they contain far too many precise, realistic details to have come from the pen of a self-indulgent novelist. In regard to Acts many radical critics betray their own historical ignorance. One could truthfully say that Paul belongs to the best-

known Jewish personalities of the first century and in this regard
is not second to Josephus; this we owe not only to his distinctive
letters but also to a good part of Luke's portrayal.

The Final Separation

The whole problem can be reduced to the two following questions:
When and why did a separation between mother and daughter take
place? And what split the family apart for good?

1. A first step in the direction of separation, as vividly described
by Luke in the context of Paul's missions, was the fact that the
disorderly "messianic Jews" and their pagan following among the
God-fearers were expelled from the more strictly ordered synagogue communities, went on to form independent conventicles,
and finally distinguished themselves by the good biblical term
ekklēsia. There were at first many ties, personal and customary;
there were discussions and arguments; at first it looked as if the
new, eschatological sect had only founded a new, synagogal assembly with some strange, but also many familiar, customs. One
read the old Scriptures, but with an entirely new, prophetic zeal;
one prayed according to the trusted forms, but also in the name
of Christ; one sang the same Psalter, but now along with christological hymns; one lived according to the same ethical commands
of the Scriptures, but now with emphasis upon the commandment
of love; one abhorred idolatry and pagan vices, and so forth. It is
furthermore probable that some Jewish Christians continued to go
to the synagogues, say, on great feast days, while also going to the
new, eschatological conventicles. Indeed, Paul warns only that one
be careful in dealing with pagans and their sacrificial meals, saying nothing against invitations from Jewish friends and relatives.
At this time, no one was thinking about the future, historical fate
of one's own religion or confession but rather looking toward the
coming parousia of Christ, which would openly reveal God's truth,
resolve all open questions, and bring an end to the momentary conflicts and eschatologically motivated separation. One could say that
the burning expectation of Christ's return kept the separation of
time from running its inevitable course.

2. An essential factor in this development was the destruction of Jerusalem in 70, which prevented the city from being the further center of the new movement. But the first sharp break between Jews and Jewish Christians was already made when James, the Lord's brother and head of the original community of the holy city, was stoned along with other Jewish Christians as alleged transgressors of the law around 62, an event that transpired under the direction of Annas (Ananus) II, the son of the Annas of the passion narrative who was the head of the Sadducees. Interestingly enough, the Pharisees, King Agrippa II, and the officiating procurator Albinus subsequently deposed Annas for having committed an illegal act of violence against a Ḥasid named "the righteous," which would seem to make it clear that these Jewish Christians were in no way subversive, politically dangerous revolutionaries. Shortly thereafter, Peter and Paul were executed in Rome, presumably during the Neronian persecution in 64. It is furthermore possible that John, the son of Zebedee, was also stoned in Jerusalem; for according to a note of Papias, both James and his brother John were killed "by the Jews" (James was executed by Agrippa I in 43, and the fact that John was martyred before 70 can be deduced from Mark 10:38–39). This would mean that of the five leading figures of the original church, three were killed in Jerusalem and two in Rome.

Shortly thereafter, presumably at the outbreak of war in 66, a significant part of the original community is reported to have fled to Pella on the basis of a revelation, and there is no reason to doubt these reports. Even if a remnant returned to the city after its destruction (an event which, according to Hegesippus, Origen, and Eusebius, the Jewish Christians considered to be a punishment for the execution of James, "the righteous") and even if, according to Epiphanius, they had established a small new church in a house on the southern end of the western hill, the Jewish Christian communities had lost the considerable influence they previously had upon the other churches of the Diaspora and were in time erased from the scene in Judea with the Bar Kochba revolt. Even the community in the new establishment of Aelia Capitolina was from its beginnings a Gentile Christian community.

3. It is all the more conspicuous that the New Testament texts leave behind no obvious or substantial traces of the city's total de-

struction by the Romans; when it is mentioned, it is mentioned only in passing. This is true of Matthew, Luke, and John, as well as Revelation. As for Mark, it is my opinion that it was written merely in expectation shortly before the destruction. Luke provides the clearest information since he was writing shortly thereafter, presumably between 75 and 80. It is also rather interesting that the New Testament does not interpret the catastrophe as one finds in later writings, namely, as a clear form of punishment for Israel's unbelief and the execution of Jesus. But even if the Jewish Christian community came to lose its authority, Luke, Matthew, and even Revelation all continue to evince a strong interest in Eretz Yisrael and the holy city, an interest that clearly points back to traditions before 70. The city's destruction may have been viewed as a form of divine judgment (as in 4 Ezra and certain rabbinic sources), and it may be related that Jesus lamentingly foresaw its fate. But the event was never given strong polemical emphasis; in this context one finds no traces of Christian triumphalism, only feelings of regret and even horror. Matthew 27:25, a verse that is strongly criticized today as an allegedly anti-Semitic text, refers indirectly to the catastrophe that befell the Jewish people between 66 and 73, a period that saw the death of innumerable Jews, who were not only killed during fighting in Galilee and Judea itself but also in the surrounding Palestinian and southern Syrian cities, in Alexandria, and even in the arenas of Antioch and Rome. These horrors clearly shook Jewish Christianity as well; for, though it had never formed a strict unity — just as Judaism itself — it had until this time played the leading role. But the catastrophe that befell Palestinian Judaism was not the main cause of separation.

4. Another factor that has been the subject of much discussion but should not be overstated is the relatively quick consolidation of Judaism in Eretz Yisrael itself, which occurred under the leadership of peace-seeking Pharisees and involved the gradual expulsion of nonconforming Jewish groups — a step that was more or less necessary in order to bring about the cessation of divisions and conflicts in Israel and therewith the religious and political restoration of the people. With this turn of events, the Sadducees, the Boethusians, the Essenes, and the Zealots all disappear from history, and the Jewish Christians are pushed into separation along with certain Gnostic groups about which we often know nothing

more than their names. More and more, the former pluralism gave
way to the pursuit of unity, to a period of consolidation, which began with quick success, was interrupted by the Bar Kochba revolt,
and ended with the redaction of the Mishna at the beginning of
the third century; this effected a deep change in Judaism that has
stamped its further history up until the reforms of the nineteenth
century and even until today.

One might therefore express the relationship between Judaism
and Christianity not only as one between mother and daughter
but also as one between two siblings that have grown increasingly
apart. The first clear sign of this development, which is manifest in
the late writings of the New Testament, is to be found in the Gospel of Matthew, which was written by a Jewish Christian scribe
(c. 90 and 95) and contains a stereotypical polemic against the
"scribes and Pharisees" — whereby one notices the diminishing
importance of the Sadducees, who by this time had probably disap-
peared. Written in a mixed community not far from Eretz Yisrael,
it clearly testifies to the early predominance of Jewish Christians
and consciously limits Jesus' activity with but two exceptions to Israel. (Indeed, it is first the resurrected Jesus who commissions the
disciples to bring the gospel to all peoples.) It expresses, furthermore, by its polemic and its emphasis on Jesus' relation to God's
people, the nature of the conflict at the end of the first century. In
the Johannine corpus (the Gospel and the letters), however, which
was likewise written by a Jewish Christian and most likely edited in
the first years of the second century, the rift is even wider and the
mutual dislike — not to say hatred — even greater. In spite of all
the Jewish Palestinian tradition it contains, it was almost certainly
written in a Gentile Christian milieu, most probably in Asia Minor,
where it also came to have its greatest influence. I have already
mentioned some of the causes of separation as well as some of the
remaining things in common, but there is also a real proximity to
Judaism that is attested by a passage from the third letter of John:
those sent out by the "old one" (John) as missionaries of Christ
accepted no support, that is, neither food nor housing, "from the
Gentiles," apparently because of the fear that they would be made
unclean by such association. Perhaps one has to do here with certain aftereffects of the apostolic decree, but originally one does
not find such conscious separation anywhere but among Jews and
law-abiding Jewish Christians.

5. The main reason for the separation, or better put, the growing apart, has to do with a generational shift. First it must be said, however, that even though Paul views circumcision as a merely ethnic distinction, no longer having any significance for salvation, he himself does not forbid Jewish Christians from circumcising their children; in fact, he saw to the circumcision of his chosen missionary companion, Timothy, the son of a Jewish mother and a pagan father (Acts 16:1–3), in order to reprove accusations that he was teaching apostasy and to keep the missionary door to the synagogues open. The question here, however, is whether the Jewish Christians who were a minority in the Pauline and other Gentile Christian communities continued to adhere to the ritual law and have their children circumcised. According to Acts 21:21, radical Jewish Christians (and above all Jewish opponents) made the following accusation against Paul: "They had been told about you that you teach all the Jews living among the Gentiles to forsake Moses, and that you tell them not to circumcise their children or observe the customs." Objectively speaking, this was clearly false, for as his letters attest, Paul had only forbidden the circumcision of pagans but never directly hindered the circumcision of Jewish Christians. At most, he emphasized its insignificance in respect to the disposition of one's heart.

Nonetheless, the accusation did point to a tendency that was long in effect. For the Gentile Christian communities were more and more inclined to emphasize the distance between them and the synagogue and vice versa. For example, from the second half of the first century onward, the messianic liturgy was celebrated on the day of the Messiah's resurrection, and the simpler codex was used for liturgical readings in place of the scrolls of holy Scripture. This indicates that the new communities wanted to distinguish themselves from the traditional liturgy of the synagogue even in regard to external form, even if, according to our earliest example in Justin Martyr, they retained the basic prayers, the liturgical readings, and the sermon as part of the service prior to the celebration of the Eucharist. By the time of the second and third generation there were only a few Jewish Christian groups at the fringe of the church that were still observing the ritual law. This remains true even if several communities in Asia Minor and Syria continued to hold to the compromises of the apostolic council, which (contrary to Luke) was most likely intended to settle the conflict adumbrated by Paul in Galatians 2:11–12. Even for Jewish Christians in the predominantly Gentile Christian communities of the Diaspora in the Roman Empire, such things as circumcision, the sabbath, dietary law, and yearly feast days were for the most part no longer observed after the second half of the first century, unless they went on to organize their own messianic conventicles. Even so, it is clear from Justin and Irenaeus that Jewish Christianity still had a certain importance; indeed, Justin concedes to this group a privileged existence, so long as they do not demand that Gentile Christians also observe the Mosaic law. But even the letter of James (which comes out of a Jewish Christian milieu, contains a clear, anti-Pauline slant, and was possibly written by James himself), already desists from all references to ritual law. For the "perfect law of freedom" implies not ritual but ethical commands.

6. Rather than speaking of the growing apart in the mild terms of a generational shift, however, one could also speak of a progressive estrangement that made the rift gradually unbridgeable and was conditioned by the phenomena mentioned, namely, the destruction of Jerusalem, the gradual consolidation of Judaism (above all in Palestine and Syria), the expulsion of Jewish Christians from the synagogue, and Jewish Christianity's concurrent loss of predominance. At this point, mother and daughter no longer had much to say to one another, the relationship was mutually broken off, and there were fewer and fewer discussions and arguments. Even if there were certain points of agreement, for example, in such passages as Romans 9–11 or even John 4:22, which find an echo on the Jewish side, say, in the counsel of Gamaliel (Acts 5:38) or in the protest of the Pharisees against the execution of James, these too faded out by the turn of the century. This is especially true to the extent that the young Christian communities were influenced by radical Gnostic groups and prompted by them into a fundamental critique of the Old Testament and its picture of God as Creator and Lord of history. In my opinion, this new, Gnostic movement had both Jewish Hellenistic and Platonic roots and is to be traced back to religiously homeless Jewish Samaritan intellectuals who had attached themselves to the church and, in particular, their reaction to the catastrophe of 70. They adopted a Christian understanding of redemption but without the offense of the incarnation and crucifixion of the Son of God. This provides

for a conflict with Ignatius, who in his polemics shows himself to be the first author of a purely Gentile Christianity.

7. Although there are no clear indications in the sources, a minor part in this development could also have been played by the *fiscus Iudaicus*, the Jewish didrachma tax paid to Jupiter Capitolinus in Rome, which followed along the lines of the old temple tax and was introduced by Vespasian after 70. It may have given Jewish Christians who were no longer observing the ritual law a sufficient reason not to circumcise their children and even encouraged them to disclaim their standing as Jews. Apparently, the tax was most rigorously collected under Domitian, who even succeeded in arousing opposition from parts of the Roman nobility. This ultimately brought his successor Nerva to do something most unusual, namely, mint coins with the inscription *Calumnia fisci Iudaici sublata* (an act that brought to an end the false accusations that had been made against the Jews in light of the tax).

In Matthew 17:24–27 this question is addressed in a legend of Peter which, judging from its content, can be traced back to the old temple tax and possibly even to an instruction of Jesus himself. Though the "sons of the kings" are in essence exempted from the tax, one should still pay it, "so that we may not offend them" (Matt. 17:27). Because this instruction for Jewish Christians could also be understood to apply to the *fiscus Iudaicus*, it is possible that the issue of this taxation, which was ever leading to conflict anyway, could also have ended up accelerating the separation of ways. For the descendants of Jewish Christians likewise wanted nothing more to do with a tax that was collected from circumcised Jews.

8. It is here worth noting a historical example that has been the subject of much discussion. Even during the reign of Domitian, one can see how difficult it was to distinguish between Jews and Christians. This is particularly true in regard to the old conflict surrounding Titus Flavius Clemens, who was Domitian's cousin and potential successor, and his wife Flavia Domitilla, the emperor's niece. According to Dio Cassius (67.14.1–2), Domitian executed Titus along with other sympathizers on account of Judaizing inclinations and then banished his wife Flavia Domitilla to the island Pandeteria. The decisive passage reads as follows: "In the same year Domitian executed the consul Flavius Clemens along with

many others, even though he was his cousin and Flavia Domitilla, with whom he was related, was his wife. Both were accused of being godless (*engklēma atheotētos*), and upon this same basis many others were condemned for having fallen into Jewish customs (*es ta tōn Ioudaiōn ēthē exokellontes*). Of these some were killed, and some were at the very least robbed of their possessions." Eusebius (*Ecclesiastical History* 3.18.4) reports, on the other hand, that Flavia Domitilla was banished with many others to the island of Pontia "on account of her witness to Christ." In my opinion, the question has to remain inconclusive whether the relatives of Domitian had fallen away to Judaism or to Christianity, for Dio Cassius, who was writing around the first third of the third century, was not ignorant of the Christians; rather, he hated them, even to the point of excluding their mention by a *damnatio memoriae* from all his works. So it is not to be expected that he would call them by name, particularly in this delicate context; in fact, he gives no more concrete description of their bad superstition than the elliptical words *ta tōn Ioudaiōn ēthē*. It therefore remains an open question to what extent the couple, who were both descendants of Vespasian, and next to the emperor had the highest position in the empire, had involved themselves in Jewish or Christian "superstition." In the absence of any new sources, the puzzle will remain insoluble. Finally, if we are to believe Eusebius (*Ecclesiastical History* 3.20.1–6, quoting Hegesippus), even the great-nephews of Jesus, whom Domitian had brought to Rome for presentation, were not brought as Christians but as Jewish descendants of David; nonetheless they were questioned by Domitian regarding their Jewish Christian superstition and, unlike the members of the imperial family and the senatorial nobility, were released with an expression of contempt and sent home as simple peasants and taxpayers.

9. Thus, even after their separation, which becomes definitive in the first decades of the second century, the relationship between Jews and Christians remained special — one could even say unique. It was bonded, among other things, by the possession of the holy Scriptures; accordingly, the Hebrew Bible provided the basis of orientation for the first Christian canon of the Old Testament, which Melito of Sardis brought back from his pilgrimage to the Holy Land. During the debate within the church concerning the extent of inspired writings and the scope of the Old Testament, an im-

portant argument for a smaller canon and therewith the rejection of apocryphal and pseudepigraphal writings remained the fact that the Hebrew Bible itself was smaller, whereby the number of letters, the twenty-two consonants of the Hebrew alphabet, likewise remained a model. In the end the larger canon of the Septuagint and the Latin Bible, which is dependent upon it, represented a sort of compromise.

Nor is it a coincidence that we know of two literary dialogues from the second century between a Christian and a Jew, but of none between Christians and pagans. As for *Octavius*, the Latin dialogue of Minucius Felix, it belongs well within the third century; and as for the antinomians like the Simonians, Carpocrates, Cerdo, and Marcion would have found such dialogues between Christians and Jews meaningless. Even later on, the polemical writings *adversus Iudaeos* remained at least as common as those against pagan superstitions; likewise, Christian apologetical polemics against pagan intellectuals and idolatry are essentially but continuations of the old Jewish apologetics, as one finds, for example, in Josephus's *Contra Apionem*. Like Josephus, one appealed to the age of the biblical-prophetic tradition, moreover, to the Creator and Lord to whom it bears witness, the Lord not only of the salvation history of Israel but of the entire history of the world. At a fundamental level the apologetic was therefore concerned with the Septuagint and Christianity's relation to the Jews; as such, it was common to have a certain love for and familiarity with the Hellenistic Jewish literary tradition, which was ignored by the rabbinical teachers of Palestine, therewith rejected, and soon forgotten. For Christians, however, it remained a tradition in which one believed to find, as the title of Eusebius of Caesarea's learned work indicates, a *praeparatio evangelica*.

The pagan opponents of Christianity, like Celsus, Porphyry and Julian the Apostate, were always given to emphasizing the connection rather than the difference between Judaism and Christianity, viewing the latter as an even worse form of superstition. For, being a national religion, Judaism could always underscore its own venerable age. Yet, in spite of the hatred, the oppression that began with Theodosius at the end of the fourth century, and the persecution of the Jews in and following the Crusades, the sense of a unique connection essentially remained. One was always conscious of being related, even and precisely when emphasizing fundamental differences — after all, the Old Testament of the Septuagint did constitute the larger part of holy Scripture. Indeed, the Christians never really got away from Judaism. There always remained a latent interest, and moreover, one that did not always prove to be negative but has also been positive time and again. Throughout christological and trinitarian interpretation, the fundamental "one Lord" of Deuteronomy 6:4 (cf. Mark 12:29) remained identical with the one God, the Creator of the world and the Lord of salvation history.

Some Conclusions

Without being able to foresee the consequences it may have for both religions, the possibility of unbiased research, which has gradually opened up since the Enlightenment and led in the last fifty years to greater mutual understanding, brings with it the possibility of considerable historical and theological enrichment for both Christians and Jews alike. I would like to summarize the results of the foregoing in the following points.

1. It is generally recognized that a knowledge of Judaism from this time period is essential to scholarship of the beginnings of Christianity and to the interpretation of the New Testament. Furthermore, relating the beginnings of Christianity to the context of Jewish history of that period constitutes an essential enrichment that allows us better to understand the creative energy of Jewish thought at that time, for even an illegitimate daughter has decisive features in common with her mother.

2. Next to Josephus, Philo, Qumran, and the early rabbinic tradition, the New Testament could become the most important source for a knowledge of first-century Judaism. Viewed historically, it is the most important offspring of Judaism and, as I see it, represented one of several real possibilities within the development of Judaism in antiquity.

3. Jewish research interest should not limit itself to such an exceptional figure as Jesus of Nazareth but also include the corpus Paulinum, the Acts of the Apostles, the corpus Johanneum, indeed,

cum grano salis, even the Gnostic texts and the Fathers of the second century up to Clement of Alexandria and Tertullian. Directly or indirectly, these texts illumine the conceptions and motives of contemporary Judaism; moreover, as Origen and Jerome show, the discussion between Jews and Christians continued even in later centuries.

4. This concerns not only comparative religious studies but also, in part, social and political history. Just as parts of the Gospels and Acts are more easily understood in light of Josephus, so can the former be a source of confirmation to the latter — at times correcting, at times supplementing, in any event so as to make a deeper understanding possible. In relation to this issue, I have just written an article on the Gospel of John as a source for ancient Judaism. If I may, I would like to quote the historian of antiquity Fergus Millar: "The world of the gospels is that of Josephus" ("Reflections on the Trial of Jesus," in *A Tribute to Geza Vermes: Essays on Jewish and Christian Literature and History,* ed. Philip R. Davies and Richard T. White [Sheffield: JSOT Press, 1990], 357).

5. The goal of this mutual research of the sources should no longer be the apologetic definition and biased estimation of one's own position but the earnest understanding of classical texts of the other side, their authors and the events that they describe. At the same time, a better understanding is most possible when one does not fully shy away from one's own standpoint but expresses it in each case with the necessary clarity; for only when one strives to define one's own position can one understand and respect the different and consciously held position of others. For a person who thinks that everything should be true in the same way, truth has in effect ceased to be.

2
Paul:
Councils and
Controversies
C. K. Barrett

Historical Background of the Councils

Paul was and remains a controversial figure, and there are few
better ways of getting at both the man and his thought than by
examining the story of the controversies in which he was engaged.
It might exaggerate a little to say that these focus upon the great
council in which he and Barnabas, with James, Cephas, and John,
took part. It is true that this occupies a more than arithmetically
central place in Acts, but in this there may be a measure of artifi-
ciality. Luke is using on the grand scale one of his favorite narrative
forms: a problem arises, the problem is solved, and in addition a
great expansion of the church results. It is so here. The council is
caused by the first Christian steps outside Judaism, and it leads to
and provides the framework for the great expansion of the church
into the Gentile world. Luke's account is to a great extent true,
in that the council provided the lines on which the church was
to grow, but there is something in the suggestion that Luke, who
knew these lines well, produced them backwards in time so as to
create, or at least to formulate, his council story. Be that as it may,
we know that the council was important to Paul, and I propose to
begin not with Acts 15 but with Galatians 2.

I am assuming that Acts 15 and Galatians 2 are related to the
same sequence of events. J. B. Lightfoot's argument — the geogra-
phy is the same, the time is the same, the persons are the same,
the subject of dispute is the same, the character of the conference

is in general the same, the result is the same — needs a certain amount of qualification, as we shall see, but it carries a good deal of weight. The Jerusalem visit of Acts 11:30 and 12:25 need not trouble us.

We may then attend to Galatians 2. Verses 1 and 2 set the stage and emphasize the importance of the event. The wrong result could have undone Paul's work and brought his mission to an end. Not because disagreement would have proved him wrong — it would for him only have proved his opponents wrong. But it could have destroyed his churches, cutting them off from their roots in the life, death, and resurrection of Jesus, centered as these were in Jerusalem. So he came to see what the Jerusalem authorities — *hoi dokountes* is what he calls them, but for the present I forbear to translate the word — made of his gospel. It was, as he had already said (Gal. 1:6–7), the only gospel there is, though there were those who preached a bogus gospel.

These had to be dealt with first, and, unlike the acknowledged authorities, were the real enemy. Paul has hard words for them. They were false brothers, not genuine Christians at all. They had no right to be there; they had gate-crashed the party — thus they were *pareisaktoi* ("secretly brought in") and *pareisēlthon* ("they slipped in," Gal. 2:4). They had come to spy (*kataskopēsai;* the word implies deceitful proceedings). And they wished to have Titus, a representative Gentile Christian, circumcised. To this demand Paul uttered a clear no; not for a moment would he tolerate the plan. Salvation is of God's grace, free and unconditional; God was the God of Gentiles as well as of Jews. The truth of the gospel must be secured (Gal. 2:5).

So much for the false brothers; Paul turns to those whom he had come to consult, notably James, Cephas, and John. It is clear that he had no high opinion of them. The word that is characteristic of 2:1–10 is *dokein:*

verse 2, *tois dokousin,* "to those of repute"

verse 6, *tōn dokountōn einai ti,* "those reputed to be something"

verse 6, *hoi dokountes,* "those of repute"

verse 9, *hoi dokountes styloi einai,* "those reputed to be pillars"

With these, and especially with verse 6, we must compare Galatians 6:3, *ei gar dokei tis einai ti mēden ōn, phrenapata heauton*
("if anyone thinks himself to be something when he is nothing, he
is deceiving himself"). This determines the meaning; *dokein* here
refers not to the opinion of others, as it may do in other passages, but to the opinion of the persons in question. It is clear
that it is used ironically. This appears as Paul's attitude in the par-
enthetical clause in 2:6, *hopoioi pote ēsan ouden moi diapherei·
prosōpon ho theos anthrōpou ou lambanei* ("whatever they were
makes no difference to me; God shows no partiality"). They may
think themselves to be something, to be the pillars on which God's
eschatological temple will stand. But Paul is not impressed. He had
met them before (1:18–19, Cephas and James). They are, however, people with whom he can talk, with whom he can make an
agreement. They recognized the grace that had been given to Paul
(v. 9), that he belonged within the Christian fold and had been
equipped for a specific ministry (v. 7). God who had given Peter an
apostolate (*apostolē*) to the circumcision had given Paul an apostolate (but they do not use the word — is this an accident?) to
the uncircumcision (v. 8). There was a gospel for each division of
humankind (v. 7). Did this run counter to 1:6–7? Not necessarily;
perhaps what they meant was that the one gospel took different
forms when presented to different people. So the agreement was
struck: *hēmeis eis ta ethnē, autoi de eis tēn peritomēn* (v. 9: "we
to the Gentiles, they to the circumcision"). This was essentially an
agreement to differ. We will go on doing what we are doing; you
can go on doing what you have been doing. We shall not interfere, and (as silence shows) we shall not expect Gentile converts
to be circumcised. Gentiles will still be Gentiles, and Jews will still
be Jews.

It was an agreement; a compromise agreement. Its weaknesses
are already apparent. Was Paul an apostle, or not? Are there two
gospels? If Paul's gospel is true, the whole gospel is for the whole
world; who has the right to say Jews only, or Gentiles only? And
there was another problem just below the horizon: if Jews were
won by their gospel and Gentiles by theirs, how were Jewish converts to be related to Gentile converts? We shall meet this problem
in due course. Still, it was an agreement; and Paul could, and did,
go on doing what he had been doing before.

What we must at this point observe is that Paul the controversialist has to operate on two levels: against an enemy, the false brothers, who are to be found not only in Jerusalem but also on the ground in Galatia, needing to be fought tooth and nail; and against half-hearted friends, who if they had been really in agreement would have been working — and fighting — at his side. In fact, Paul must have often been uncertain whether or not they were secretly aiding the false brothers. This duality is of vital importance for the understanding of Paul's controversies. It can be observed in letter after letter.

From the Corinthian letters we can learn what was for Paul the key issue. In 1 Corinthians 15:11 Paul says, "whether then it is I or they, so we preach and so you believed." This statement is sometimes given a fuller meaning than it will bear. Paul is in this chapter arguing about resurrection, and in this verse he makes the point that there is no Christian preaching that does not include the resurrection of Jesus. This will take us further. You cannot believe in the resurrection of a crucified man if you cannot find some interpretation of his death. Such an interpretation appears in 15:3–4, in a pre-Pauline and therefore very old preaching tradition: Christ died for our sins according to the Scriptures, and he was buried, and on the third day he was raised up according to the Scriptures. If Cephas and James preach this — and their names appear among the eyewitnesses (it is because they believed it that others do) — they are proclaiming what Paul can recognize as the one gospel. They may not make as much of "for our sins" and "according to the Scriptures" as Paul does, but they are on the same side. So in 1 Corinthians we can see the half-friends — on this occasion perhaps three-quarters friends. Their preaching is right, and they are acceptable.

What of the enemies? There is not much sign of them in 1 Corinthians; in chapters 1–4 Peter comes off less well than Apollos and there may be an unfavorable reference to the notion that he was the foundation stone, or pillar, of the church (3:11), but he is on the right side. But 9:2 shows that there were some who did not regard Paul as an apostle; so does 15:9; he was an *ektrōma*, "one untimely born" (15:8). Moreover, there were those in Corinth who thought it wrong to eat *eidōlothyta*, food sacrificed to idols. They did not learn this from their pagan background or from Paul. It must have come from Jewish influence, perhaps Jewish Christian, and perhaps formulated by the decree of Acts 15:29 (on which see below). See also 1 Corinthians 7:19; Paul found it necessary to point out that circumcision was of no importance.

In many ways the situation in Corinth had changed when 2 Corinthians was written. It now becomes clear that strangers had entered the church from without and poisoned its relation with Paul. There were others, however, whom Paul treats with nothing worse than the irony he had used on those who thought themselves to be pillars; indeed these must be the same persons, though now they are described as *hyperlian apostoloi,* "superapostles" (2 Cor. 11:5; 12:11). Paul claims to be their equal in status and origin (Hebrew, Israelite, descendant of Abraham) and their superior in the sufferings he has endured in the service of Christ (11:22–23). These are not the enemy; some do not distinguish the two groups, but I think we must. There are false apostles, deceitful workers, servants of Satan. You cannot say of people like that, I think I am as good as they are (2 Cor. 11:5; 12:11); it is with reference to the *hyperlian apostoloi* that Paul says this. The false apostles are, to Paul's sorrow, welcomed by the Corinthians. They preach a different gospel (this is the absolute criterion), another Jesus, a different Spirit (11:4). They invade other men's territory, and boast of labors not performed by themselves (10:14–16). They launch a disparaging attack on Paul; he knows, they say, how to write strong letters, but his presence is feeble (10:10). They or others of the same kind dilute and pollute the gospel (2:17); they arm themselves with commendatory letters (3:1). Paul's problem is to know what connection, if any, there is between the two groups. Are the *hyperlian apostoloi* entirely innocent of the activities of the *pseudapostoloi?* Or do they, perhaps secretly, support them? Who has written the commendatory letters that they use? Did Paul know? Did he guess? It may have occurred to him that once an envoy, in ancient times, had passed out of the sight of the one who commissioned him the latter had no control over him. Not only could he say and do what he pleased; he could attribute what he pleased to his employer. On such matters one can only speculate; what is beyond speculation is that the Corinthian letters, like Galatians, bear witness to a two-level opposition to Paul and his mission.

There is more evidence to collect. Some of the evidence provided by Philippians concerns Philippi, other evidence the place in which the epistle was written. This may have been Rome, Ephesus, or Caesarea. I cannot discuss the question here; I prefer Rome, but the other possibilities should be kept in mind. The same twofold opposition appears.

In Philippians 1 Paul speaks of those who preach out of envy and strife (vv. 15, 17), thinking to add to the imprisoned apostle's troubles — his imprisonment provides us with an opportunity to add to our reputation as preachers and to gain disciples for our outlook and understanding of Christian truth; that will upset him! They are mistaken; for Paul, what matters is that for whatever reason, with whatever motive, Christ is being preached; and "therein I rejoice" (v. 18). Here are people who, in the realm of ecclesiastical politics, wish to injure Paul, but they are preaching Christ, using it may be words like those of 1 Corinthians 15:3–4. This to Paul was the only gospel there was, and these men were preaching it. There is no question here of preaching "another Jesus," a "different gospel" (2 Cor. 11:4); hence no room for the anathemas of Galatians 1:8–9.

It is disputed whether the two passages in Philippians 3 that refer to troublemakers deal with disturbances happening in Philippi or are warnings of trouble that may be feared. For our purpose this is of no importance. Paul speaks of troublemakers whom he knows to exist; whether they have reached Philippi or are still on the way is of no account. In both passages Paul speaks as sharply and vehemently as anywhere in his letters. In 3:2–3 the readers are warned against teachers who are evidently circumcised Jews, who wish presumably to have the Gentile Christians of Philippi circumcised. They are described in a way that recalls and perhaps exceeds 2 Corinthians 11. They are "dogs"; they are "evil workers"; they are given the insulting title *katatomē* ("those who mutilate"), while Paul reserves the word *peritomē* ("circumcision") for himself and his fellow Christians, whom he considers to bear the true marks of the people of God. These opponents have confidence in the flesh, that is, in the literal circumcision that they have. This leads to an important statement of the righteousness that comes from the law and the righteousness that comes by faith.

At the end of the chapter there is a further warning, this time against adversaries who are described as enemies of the cross of Christ, whose end is perdition, whose god is their belly, and whose glory is in their shame (Phil. 3:18–19). It is not clear whether this is a second reference to those mentioned at the beginning of the chapter or whether it deals with a different group. The earlier reference is undoubtedly to Jews or rather to Jewish Christians. The later passage seems at first to refer to liberals in theology: they have no room in their thought for the cross of Christ; and to libertines in morals: they are gluttons and they boast of their shameful behavior. A strong case, however, can be made for the view that they also are Judaizers. Their interest in what they put into their bellies, in what they eat, amounts to idolatry; that means, perhaps, not that they are epicures and gluttons but that they hold fast to food laws. Their shame, *aischynē,* could refer to the male sexual organ. There is evidence for this use of the word in the Liddell and Scott lexicon, but most important is the evidence of the Septuagint, where sometimes (not always) the Greek word renders ʿerᵉwāh often of female pudenda (but see Isa. 20:4; Ezek. 22:10 for ʿerᵉwāh / aischynē of the male). The word may point to the location and thus to the act and state of circumcision, in which they boast. These things recall Galatians 5:11; 6:12–13. Those who wish the Galatians to be circumcised do so in order that they may not be persecuted for the cross of Christ; their intention also is to "glory in your flesh," in that part of your flesh in which circumcision is carried out; one might say that their glory is in the shame (*aischynē*).

If these observations are valid it could well be that Philippians 3:2–3 and 3:18–19 refer to the same people, to Judaizers. This would be interesting, but whether it is correct or not we may note that in Philippians, as in Galatians and the Corinthian letters, we have to distinguish between two levels of opposition. There is the opposition to which Paul is prepared to give the benefit of the doubt, not simply out of charity but because, whatever its motives may be, it does preach the one gospel of Christ crucified and risen. This is a party with which he can enter into agreement, even though he may have reason to suspect that it tolerates if it does not support the second kind of opposition, which preaches a gospel that is no gospel and would, if unchecked, destroy the work that he is doing. It was a complicated controversial situation that formed the framework of Paul's mission, and Paul can hardly have been unaware that the agreements he was able to make were unstable and insecure.

Is there more evidence for this twofold opposition? It is worthwhile to note in Romans the sensitive way in which Paul handles the relation between the weak and the strong. There is no question that Paul himself is one of the strong (14:14; 15:1). He does not think that a vegetarian diet will commend him to God. It is by faith only and not by the observance of dietary laws that he stands before God. But if the weak should not judge the omnivorous strong, neither should the strong despise the weak (14:10). That is, Paul gives full allowance to the weak to maintain their position and their practices. He who does not eat, to the Lord he does not eat, and he gives God thanks (Rom. 14:6). Each of us will give account to God (14:12); all may and should live together in peace. The weak do come somewhere near to perverting the gospel of *sola gratia* and *sola fide* but maintain something of the *solus Christus,* and that is enough. The only place in Romans where there may be a glimpse of the radical opponents of Paul is in chapters 9–11, where Paul argues that it is right to pursue the Gentile mission because when the fullness of the Gentiles has been included in the people of God all Israel will be saved (11:25–26). This may be intended as a counterblast to a Jewish Christian belief that all Israel must be saved first and that only then will it be legitimate to embark on a mission to the Gentiles. There will be more about this when eventually we look at Acts 15. But James and Cephas seem to have thought that the two missions could be pursued side by side (Gal. 2:9), a view with which Paul does not disagree.

It is probable that 1 Thessalonians is the earliest extant Pauline letter; for our purpose there is little that we can learn from it. What we may observe is Paul's repudiation of flattery, of a concealed plan to exploit, of a desire to seek personal glory (2:5–6). "We [himself and Silas?] might have made ourselves a burden (*en barei einai*) to you as apostles of Christ, but instead we were gentle among you" (2:7). This may reflect the notion, which if it existed will have had some cause, even if the cause arose out of a misunderstanding, that apostles were expected to be authoritarian, a charge that Paul brings or implies against his opponents — perhaps the pillars, the *hyperlian apostoloi.* These apostles thought it proper to fulfill their office by lording it over the members of their churches, whereas Paul thought of himself as his people's slave (2 Cor. 1:24; 4:5); there is only one *kyrios,* as there is only one foundation. All this is consistent with what is written in 1 Thessalonians, but it cannot stand on its own as independent interpretation of the text of the epistle. It is only because we have evidence elsewhere of this authoritarian attitude that we may suspect it in Thessalonica.

To resume: it seems impossible to avoid the conclusion that the evidence collected from the epistles points clearly to the existence of two kinds of troublemakers in the Pauline churches. It is important to keep the distinction in mind not least because it brings out so clearly the importance in Paul's thought and practice of preaching. If this is right, a good deal of variety can be tolerated. "Let each one be fully convinced in his own mind" (Rom. 14:5, taken in the whole context). If it is not right, nothing can be right. There are then those who are perhaps better described as unhelpful friends than as adversaries. The authorities in Jerusalem believed in and proclaimed a crucified and risen Jesus; they were the origin and support of this proclamation. They saw in his work the forgiveness of sins. This fundamental faithfulness to what he too understood as the gospel covered for Paul a multitude of sins. On occasion, even Peter and by implication James might meet with rebuke; they met with no subservience. But they did not preach another Jesus, a different gospel, though Peter's position sometimes appears doubtful; he may perhaps sometimes have allowed himself to be drawn in on the wrong side (see below).

There was a wrong side, of those who, to adopt for Christian use the Jewish phrase, "denied the root." There is no doubt what was Paul's attitude to them. This second group was marked by a good deal of variety. Most demanding were those in Galatia and at Philippi who demanded the circumcision of Gentile converts (cf. Acts 15:1, 5). Whether this was to them the most important feature of the law we cannot be certain, but it probably was, for it was the way into Judaism, an indispensable first step. In Galatia they probably expected also observance of the sabbath and other festivals (Gal. 4:10): circumcision and the sabbath were the clearest marks of the Diaspora Jew. Perhaps they insisted on a third socially distinguishing feature, the laws of cleanness and uncleanness and other dietary laws; no doubt they approved of the separation described in Galatians 2:12–13. This was a heavy demand, but it is clear that they did not ask for observance of the whole law; they exposed themselves to Paul's criticism that anyone who gets himself circumcised is under obligation to perform the whole law (Gal. 5:3). He intends that all should recognize that the problem was not a mere matter of circumcision and nothing more.

At or near the other extreme were those who formulated and propagated the decree of Acts 15:29 (to which I shall come later).

This required only the most basic Judaism: little more than loyalty to the one God, with abstention from fornication and bloodshed. It was, however, basic Judaism that was required, and those who propagated the decree were Judaizers. There is thus a wide range of Judaizing activity, ranging from the demand for circumcision and almost, but not quite, full observance of the law to the scarcely noticeable requirements of the decree.

Another question may be raised — hardly answered — at this point. In Galatians 1:7 (cf. 4:17–18) Paul refers to "those who are troubling you (*hoi tarassontes hymas*) and wish to pervert the gospel of Christ." In 5:10 the same expression occurs in the singular, *ho tarassōn hymas*. Does this mean that the trouble in Galatia was caused by a group of Judaizers but that this group was led and could be represented by a single person? Or is the singular used generically to mean "anyone who troubles you"? In 5:10 the warning is given that the troublemaker will bear his judgment, "whoever he may be" (*hostis ean ē*). Unfortunately the last three words also are ambiguous. They may be generalizing and mean any troublemaker there is — there is no need to be specific — will bear his judgment (so, for example, the grammar of Blass-Debrunner-Rehkopf [293.1.2a.n.5; 303.n.1]). Others think otherwise. Thus Lightfoot (*Galatians,* 206): "whatever may be his position in the Church, however he may vaunt his personal intercourse with the Lord." Lightfoot must mean Peter, possibly James. H. Lietzmann (*Galaterbrief,* 38) is more explicit. He thinks that the agitation in Galatia was led by a respected personality ("eine angesehene Persönlichkeit"), and quotes Ed. Meyer for the suggestion that this was Peter, adding that it might have been Barnabas. A. Loisy (*Galates,* 183) thought of James, noting that Paul preferred not to name him, though he does do so in chapter 2. It is worth recalling the clause *hopoioi pote ēsan* ("whatever they were") in Galatians 2:6, in a similar context. At 5:10 the Latin *quaecumque est* (indicative) may support the view that finds here a reference to a particular person rather than a generalization. Peter and James have both already been mentioned as causing trouble at Antioch, and Paul may be saying, in veiled words, "be the troublemaker even Peter or James he will get the judgment he deserves." If one is to choose between Peter and James as the man on the spot, Peter may be preferred as the one who is known to have traveled from Jerusalem and may have been in Galatia as he had certainly been in

Antioch, whereas James may have been content to work through messengers.

There is good reason to think that Peter had been in Corinth too, and there is reason to think that the Corinthian troublemakers had a leader. But those mentioned in 1 Corinthians 1:11 were no more than potential leaders of division, though Apollos was a closer partner to Paul than Peter. The bearing of 1 Corinthians 9:5 is unclear. There is more material in 2 Corinthians. In 2 Corinthians 2:5 there is a person, denoted only by *tis* ("someone"), who has "caused grief" (*lelypēken*) not so much to himself, Paul says, as to the whole community. This is presumably the person who is taken up in 7:12 as *ho adikēsas* ("he who did wrong") with a corresponding *ho adikētheis* ("he who suffered wrong"). We know neither who *ho adikēsas* was nor what he had done. It is usually supposed that *ho adikētheis* was Paul himself, who had been attacked or insulted in some way. There is no indication of doctrinal disagreement, though it is possible that such disagreement could have been the cause of personal ill feeling. Paul minimizes his own sense of hurt. He urges forgiveness, and he himself forgives. It is often supposed that Paul's opponent was a member of the Corinthian church; it is more probable that he came into the church from elsewhere. This, if correct, confirms the picture of an anti-Pauline mission circulating in Paul's churches with a view to correcting his insufficiently Jewish practice. There is more material in the last part of the letter (2 Cor. 10–13). Particularly to be noticed are the singular pronouns in 10:7, the singular verb in 10:10, the singular pronoun in 10:11, and the singular substantive participle and finite verb in 11:4. In this last-mentioned verse, the substance of the gospel is involved, for *ho erchomenos* ("he who comes" [from without?]) preaches another Jesus, and as a result of his preaching his hearers receive a different Spirit and a different gospel. Here too the words could be generic, but this does not seem probable; if this had been intended it would have been easy and natural to write *ei tis erchomenos allon Iēsoun kēryssei... kalōs anechesthe* ("if anyone comes and preaches another Jesus... you readily submit to it"). If a group of anti-Paulinists came to Corinth it would be natural though not certain that they should have a leader; he could be referred to here.

Nothing in Philippians bears on this matter. The references in chapters 1 and 3 are all in the plural except 3:4b, *ei tis dokei allos pepoithenai en sarki, egō mallon* ("if any other person thinks he has reason for confidence in the flesh, I have more") — and this is a general statement. Paul would have, if he chose to appeal to it, more ground for confidence in the flesh than anyone else.

When all the passages mentioned are surveyed, there is only one person who could be named as satisfying the evidence; this is Peter, but the suggestion cannot be made with much confidence. He is named as the leader, but probably the unwilling leader, of a group in Corinth (1 Cor. 1:12). In the same epistle (9:5) he is mentioned as one of those who made use of apostolic privileges that Paul renounced. In Galatians 2:11–15 he takes (under pressure from James) a view opposite to Paul's on the relation between Jewish and Gentile Christians. Galatians 1:18 is worth considering here. Paul visited Jerusalem *historēsai Kēphan* ("to visit Cephas"). Why? The meaning of *historēsai* has often been discussed, and the word itself is unlikely to tell us much. But we know why Paul made his second visit to Jerusalem (Gal. 2:2); it was in order that he might not have run or be running in vain. Was the first visit made for the same purpose? He saw the same people: James as well as Cephas. It seems probable that Paul already knew that Cephas and James were a potential threat to his work. It is tempting to follow Michael Goulder (*St. Paul versus St. Peter: A Tale of Two Missions* [London: SCM, 1994]) and to speak of a Petrine and a Pauline mission. But in the place where it matters, Peter stands among the pillars rather than the false brothers. It is, however, not unlikely that his attitude and his position varied. In the Gospels he appears as a somewhat unstable figure; the familiar image of the Rock, *Petros/Kepha,* probably means no more than that he was the first to confess the messiahship of Jesus. The evidence of Galatians 2:11–15 depicts him as an unstable character, and it may be that less reputable figures than James were able to sway him. It must be remembered that in the earliest decades Christians had no clear-cut dogmatic tradition to guide them. Paul was at work establishing such a tradition, but it is not surprising or blameworthy that this, and its importance, were not universally perceived. The story cannot be clear to us because the evidence is not sufficient; for other reasons it was probably less than clear to those who participated in it. In the hope of clarifying it a little we may pursue two further inquiries.

First we may continue with Galatians and examine what happened after the council described in 2:1–10. It is clear that a determined anti-Pauline campaign, which required the circumcision of all Gentile Christians, was in progress. We cannot suppose that this was confined to Galatia, though the campaigners may have concentrated their efforts there. In any case, we must assume that Paul told the story of what happened in Antioch because he believed it to be relevant to what was happening in Galatia. The existence of the Pauline churches was threatened (2:2). This provides the background against which Paul's rebuke of Peter in Antioch (2:11–15) must be understood. Paul's Gospel asserted the free and all-sufficient grace of God, operative in Christ crucified and risen; to suggest that this needed the complement of circumcision or any other legal provision was to destroy its foundation. It is evident that Peter had at first accepted the fact that to both Jews and non-Jews the decisive condition was their faith in Christ; this was what constituted them Abraham's seed, heirs in terms of promise (3:29). Jewish and Gentile Christians ate together with no regard for food laws. This harmony was disturbed by "certain people from James," who frightened Peter, followed by Barnabas and other Jewish Christians, into withdrawing from table fellowship. We do not know what the envoys from James said. It is possible that they were really false brothers (2:4), wrongly claiming the authority of James, but we note that they convinced Peter of their credentials.

James himself will hardly have revoked the agreement of 2:9, but that agreement must be interpreted by his subsequent actions. He must have said something like, "We agreed that there should be a Gentile mission, led by Paul, and that Gentile converts did not have to be circumcised; but we did not say that Jewish Christians might so far cease to be Jews as to eat meals where observance of Jewish laws was not guaranteed. Conversion does not obliterate the distinction between Jew and Gentile." This Peter accepted. Previously he had behaved (by eating non-Jewish meals) as if he were a Gentile; now he was requiring Gentiles, if they wished to eat with their Jewish Christian brothers, to behave like Jews (2:14). This was *hypokrisis* (2:13); Peter had been frightened into playing a part, though it is not impossible that Peter was reverting to what he truly believed and that it was with a bad conscience that he had been playing a part when he ate with Gentiles. The evidence about Peter provided by Acts is unclear and in part contradictory. According to Acts 10:14 he had never in the past eaten prohibited food but (after his vision and the gift of the Spirit) did eat with Cornelius (10:48; 12:3); however, Cornelius may have observed Jewish regulations. According to Acts 15:10 Peter had found these regulations intolerable and presumably had not observed them; yet in the decree he consented to the prohibition of improperly slaughtered food (15:29).

Paul begins by pointing out the inconsistency in Peter's attitude and no doubt in doing so became aware of the inadequacy of the agreement that had been reached in Jerusalem (Gal. 2:9; see above). The incident at Antioch may have ended at this point; it is often held that somewhere between Galatians 2:11 and 2:21 Paul, in writing his letter, moves from narrative to theological reflection. This may well be true. The transition from debating point to Christ-centered theology takes place in the text before us. It will be appropriate to consider it more fully when we turn from the historical to the theological aspects of Paul's controversial life. The christocentricity here achieved dominates the rest of Galatians, as it dominates Paul's thought as a whole.

Second, we turn to the alternative account of a Jerusalem council that is contained in Acts 15. It will be impossible here to discuss it in detail, but three questions will be profitable to consider.

The first is the place of Paul and Barnabas in the council. They were, according to Acts 15:2, deputed to go to Jerusalem in order to represent the Antiochene point of view in opposition to that of those who had come from Judea and maintained that it was impossible to be saved without circumcision (Acts 15:1; cf. v. 5). But the two Antiochene representatives make practically no contribution to the council (15:12). They narrate the signs and portents that God had done through them among the Gentiles, and this was not a bad practical argument: Would God have permitted, have actually performed, such acts of power and benevolence if he had disapproved of what was going on? But would Paul have been content to leave unspoken the theological argument about grace and faith and works? It seems improbable. We may note also the *esigēsen de* ("were silent") at the beginning of verse 12 and *meta de to sigēsai autous* ("after they had become silent") at the beginning of verse 13. There is a case, made for example by Rudolf Bultmann, for regarding the intervening words (v. 12) as an insertion into a narrative that did not originally contain them. Did Luke,

who certainly knew — rightly — of a council at which Peter and
James, Paul and Barnabas, had been present, introduce Paul and
Barnabas into a council story in which they played no part?

The second question arises out of the quotation of Amos 9:11–
12 ascribed in Acts 15:16–18 to James. There is a famous and
often discussed problem here. If read in the Hebrew text, Amos's
prophecy speaks of the supplanting by Israel of what is left of
Edom. This is of no use or relevance to anyone at the council.
Only if Amos is read in the Greek of the Septuagint do we hear
that the rest of humankind (those who are not Jews) shall seek the
Lord. Did James, of all people, in a conference conducted presumably in Hebrew (or in Aramaic, in which the passage from Amos is
even less usable) use an argument that depended on a Greek mis-
reading, as it probably was? It seems unlikely; there is no sign of
the *al tiqrei* formula used to introduce a deliberately chosen vari-
ant reading. This however is not all. Is James's quotation, in its
Septuagint form, relevant? Relevant to what? It may be enough to
say that James claims that this passage of the Old Testament sup-
ports Peter's assertion that God is interested in taking to himself a
people from the Gentile world. The quotation, however, includes
also a reference to the re-erection of David's tent as leading to the
incoming of the Gentiles. This could be taken in two ways. The
re-erection of David's tent could mean the vindication of David's
family in the coming and in the resurrection of his heir, the Messiah. This is something that has already happened; the mission to
the Gentiles may begin at once. Alternatively, the re-erection of
David's tent could mean the restoration of the Jewish people, that
is, to a Christian, the conversion of the Jewish people to Christ:
a successful mission to the Jews must precede the mission to the
Gentiles. This would imply that Amos 9:11–12 was a text whose
interpretation was argued about in discussions of the legitimacy of
the mission. This is the theme of the council described in Galatians 2, but it is not the theme of the council described in Acts 15,
which assumes the presence of Gentile converts and considers how
much of Judaism they should be required to accept.

This leads to the third question: the decree. I shall not here discuss its contents; it must suffice to say that it is treated throughout
Acts 15 not as a device intended to facilitate table fellowship between Jewish and Gentile Christians but as giving the conditions
on which Gentiles may be saved. The conditions furthermore may

be regarded as basic Judaism (without circumcision) and include both ethical and ceremonial provisions. It is also to be noted that it received a good deal of modification in the textual tradition, so that at times it seems to be purely ethical; the evidence is familiar and need not be related here. The evidence of Revelation 2:10, 14, 24 is also relevant and suggests a decree that forbade only fornication and the eating of sacrificial food. From Paul's letters one would never deduce that the decree existed, and it is hard to believe that he would ever have accepted it unless he met it in the form in which it simply forbade idolatry, fornication, and bloodshed and enjoined an attitude of general love and kindliness. This is not the form in which the original text of Acts represents Paul as approving and propagating it.

These questions, which are all that can be considered here, though others arise, are sufficient to show that behind the narratives contained in Acts there was a complicated sequence of events. Paul's story we may take more or less as it stands; I cannot follow the now fashionable tendency to defend the historicity of Acts by questioning the veracity of Paul. Luke seems to have built up his story out of materials that on the whole, sound in themselves, are in some respects mistakenly connected. Luke knew that there were important discussions in Jerusalem that dealt with the question of the Gentile mission and the terms on which Gentiles might be admitted to the saved people of God. He knew that Paul and Barnabas, as representatives of the church of Antioch, had taken part in such discussions, but the traditional account of a council that he had received did not refer to Paul and Barnabas. He should have drawn the conclusion that there had been two meetings, at one of which Paul and Barnabas were present whereas in the other they were not. Instead he inserted a reference (Acts 15:12) to Paul and Barnabas in the one story he had to tell. He may have supposed that only one such meeting took place, or he may have compressed the two into one to save time and space in his book.

Writing twenty or more years after the deaths of Paul, Peter, and James, at a time when a Gentile mission was almost universally accepted and Gentiles probably outnumbered Jews in the church, Luke supposed that the three martyrs (as probably all three were) had been closer to one another than they were and that they had been united in taking the gospel to the Gentile world, so that the only question that had to be solved was the relation of the Gentiles to Judaism, of the gospel to the law. Either he was ignorant of the confrontation between Peter and Paul in Antioch, or he chose to ignore it. We know that he had a different account (Acts 15:36–40) of the rupture between Paul and Barnabas. The event in Antioch marked the inevitable failure of the compromise reached at the first council, that of Galatians 2, and neither James (backed by Peter) nor Paul was in a compromising mood. The position was a serious one. The church of Antioch was split in two, and the same could have happened in every church that contained both Jewish and Gentile elements.

Another conference met; Paul was not present. It was of this second conference that Luke preserved a somewhat confused tradition; into this he introduced Barnabas and Paul, who he had reason to think had attended a council in Jerusalem. It was, however, a different group of missionaries that took part in this new council. This was the group, originally headed by Stephen, often called Hellenists, though this is not Luke's use of the word. They are perhaps better called Diaspora Jews; some of their work may be seen in the speeches of Acts 7 and 17. If Luke knew of the presence of such people he may have thought that they were represented by Paul and Barnabas. It was probably these Greek-speaking Jews who introduced the use of the Greek Old Testament, quoting Amos 9:11–12 to justify the two-pronged mission to Jews and Gentiles and devising in the so-called apostolic decree a better compromise than that of the earlier council. It was a better compromise because it was flexible, capable of modification and of application to practical circumstances, in which Gentiles out of courtesy had no wish to hurt the feelings of Jewish fellow Christians. Paul, it seems, had either to be informed or reminded of its contents on his final visit to Jerusalem (Acts 21:25), when, on one interpretation of the story, his relations with James fell to a still lower level. Perhaps only he recognized the new arrangement as a Judaizing compromise until a comparable theologian, Augustine, arose to be embarrassed by it.

Other events at this final visit cannot be discussed here. Luke's narrative leaves the reader with many questions. Paul had reached Jerusalem bearing the fruit of the collection he had made among the Gentile churches for the benefit of the poor saints in Jerusalem. What happened to the money? Was it used for the relief of poverty or for the discharge of dues incurred by men who had taken

Nazirite vows? Would Paul have associated himself with such men in the temple rite and done so in order to prove about himself a proposition that was only doubtfully true? What did the church of Jerusalem do to aid the prisoner of Christ? Why did he repeatedly find better treatment among Romans than elsewhere?

The story in which the councils play a prominent part is a complicated one, and it can be given continuity only with the aid of a few guesses; but those that have been given here seem to agree not only with one another but with such evidence as there is. It remains to look at the evidence from the point of view of theology.

Theological Issues at the Councils

History and theology are as a rule inseparable in the New Testament. Theology could not be excluded from the first part of this discussion, and the theology that will be considered in this second part arises out of and is presupposed by the history, of which a sketch is attempted above. It will be convenient, and I hope not unduly repetitious, to set out some of the main points afresh. They may appear more clearly if they are given in briefer form and without the arguments by which they were reached.

The New Testament contains two accounts of a meeting in Jerusalem. In each account the main actors or speakers are Peter (Cephas) and James, Paul, and Barnabas. Both accounts are concerned with the legitimacy, method, and basis of the mission by which Christianity spread out from Jerusalem into the Gentile world. They are not however identical. The narrative contained in Acts 15 arises out of contention in Antioch, where missionaries, including Paul and Barnabas, had won converts from the Gentile as well as from the Jewish world. Travelers from Judea had asserted that it was necessary to circumcise the Gentile converts and require them to observe the law of Moses. Only if they did this could they be saved. So important a matter could be properly discussed only in Jerusalem, and Paul and Barnabas, with others, went to Jerusalem for the purpose. The conclusion was embodied in a letter and in a decree, which laid down that circumcision and full observance of the law were not to be required, but that it was necessary that Gentiles should observe, if they were to belong to the saved people of God, certain basic Jewish requirements: they must abstain from food sacrificed to idols, from fornication, from blood, and from strangled meat. Of this decree neither Galatians nor any other Pauline letter shows any awareness.

According to Galatians 2 Paul, accompanied by Barnabas and Titus, went to Jerusalem (in consequence of a revelation) to lay before the authorities there the gospel that he was preaching among the Gentiles. The story of the visit falls into two parts. In the first Paul encounters false brothers, who wished to have the Gentile Titus and presumably all other Gentile converts circumcised. Paul is adamant in his refusal to allow this. In the second part his dealings are with James, Cephas, and John, who evidently regarded themselves as the pillars on which the church was built. Paul was not favorably impressed by their opinion of themselves but was able to reach an agreement with them. Each party recognized the other as preaching a valid gospel, Paul the gospel for the uncircumcision (who need not be circumcised), the pillars, especially Peter, the gospel for the circumcision. It was agreed that God had been at work in each mission, but Paul and his colleagues would confine themselves to the one, Peter and his colleagues to the other. In addition Paul had no hesitation in agreeing to a request to keep in mind the needs of poor Christians in Jerusalem. This was an agreement, and as such to be welcomed; but it is evident that it was essentially an agreement to differ, a compromise. Paul would continue to do what he had been doing, and so would Peter; and neither would interfere with the other. This was better than nothing, but it was by no means a whole-hearted acceptance of one gospel (cf. Gal. 1:6) intended for the whole world.

In the narrative of Galatians we see an uneasy peace and a division of the non-Pauline part of the church into two parties. So it must have seemed to Paul, not necessarily to others. Against him were on the one hand the pillars, whom elsewhere (2 Cor. 11:5; 12:11) he describes ironically as the "superapostles." He accepts them because he accepts their gospel, the proclamation of Christ crucified and risen. As witnesses they were the origin, the first preachers, and the guarantee of this gospel, and they found in it the forgiveness of sins (1 Cor. 15:1–11), though, as this passage shows, their position enabled some to sneer at Paul as an untimely birth, unworthy to be called an apostle. They failed to draw adequate inferences regarding both the breadth and the depth of their own gospel, but their adherence to it was sufficient for Paul. On the other hand there were those — false brothers, false apostles, dogs — whose gospel was no gospel at all. These were the enemy; the distinction can be observed in many parts of the Pauline corpus. They covered a considerable range of what may be described as Judaizing activity, sometimes including (for example, in Galatia) the demand for the circumcision of all Gentile converts, sometimes asking much less. There is some evidence that suggests that they had a leader, conceivably Peter, though it is more probable that his position varied; all were keen to have him on their side, and he was perhaps easily persuaded.

The council reports that we have in Acts and Galatians may refer to different aspects of one event; it seems more probable that they refer to two events, though Luke has assimilated his account by introducing the mention of Paul and Barnabas. The question of the Gentile mission may well have been raised by Paul, with Peter and James on Paul's first visit to Jerusalem (Gal. 1:18); it was discussed more fully, with the result described above on his second visit (Gal. 2:1–10). That the compromise agreement reached on this occasion was unsatisfactory was quickly displayed in the division of the church in Antioch, when the Jewish Christians, led by Peter and Barnabas, refused to eat with the uncircumcised Gentile Christians. The two gospels of Galatians 2:7 led to the existence of two churches, with no real fellowship between them. It was to remedy this situation that the council, of which we have an edited account in Acts 15, was called, and the decree (Acts 15:29), another compromise, composed. It is hard to believe that Paul accepted and propagated it, harder still to think that he had a hand in composing it. It was probably the product of a Gentile mission distinct from his, operated by Diaspora Jews who followed a line different in some respects from Paul's but increasingly influential in the later decades of the first century. They were probably responsible for the use of the Greek Old Testament in Acts 15:16–18. Acts 21:25 may mean that Paul was officially informed of the decree on his last visit to Jerusalem.

We may take up the theology of the history at the point where the first compromise agreement failed. This might work when the two missions were separate from each other, in districts that were wholly Jewish or wholly Gentile. But Antioch was mixed, both as a city and as a church. If Jews were, as James evidently wished, to stand firm as Jews, and if Gentiles refused to become Jews, the church was bound to split. Only a radically theological review of the situation could put it right.

Paul's first reaction, however, was to fasten on the change, the inconsistency, in Peter's behavior. "If you, born and bred (Lightfoot's suggestion for *hyparchōn*) a Jew, live as a Gentile and not as a Jew, how can you seek to compel Gentiles to live as Jews?" The present tense, *zēs* ("live"), is perhaps not quite fair to Peter, for he had now under pressure — perhaps threats — ceased to live as a Gentile and was presumably expressing penitence for ever having done so. But Paul's point is clear enough. Fear was compelling Peter to do something that was inconsistent not only with his past position but also with what appeared to have been his conviction; he was, for James's benefit, acting a part; and this was *hypokrisis* ("play-acting"). The word made a good debating weapon, and it fitted with all that we know of the council. Its decision regarding the missions was a compromise; the attitude of Jewish Christians to Gentile Christians, the attitude of James ("You may be Christians, but not of our sort"), was a compromise. And the compromise was dishonest and in the end unworkable, even when the Jewish Christian demand was reduced to nothing more demanding than the decree.

At this point the story could end, and perhaps did end. Most commentators agree that at some point between 2:14 and 2:21 Paul ceases to recount an event that took place in Antioch and goes on to develop his subsequent thinking on the question. For us it does not matter whether Paul developed his thought, thinking on his feet in Antioch, or took it further as he worked out his argument in writing to the Galatians. He develops the argument from a debating point — "Be consistent, man!" — to one of his most profound theological statements. In verse 15 he is still addressing Peter — *hēmeis* ("we") you and I — but he soon moves beyond this.

What was wrong with the council, with Jewish demands, with the decree, which, though not yet enacted at the time of the trouble in Antioch, was in existence when Paul wrote Galatians? It was that they left out the central figure who should have controlled the whole discussion. In the question about Paul's Gentile mission they did not say, "Christ died for the Jews, Christ died for the Greeks; therefore there is one mission to all the world, in which all play their part." They said rather, "We will go our separate ways and agree not to tread on each other's toes." When the question was about Christian fellowship, about Christians' eating and drinking together, they did not say, "We all live by the bread which is Christ's body and the wine which is his blood." They said rather, "You give up this and we will give up that." It may be that I exaggerate somewhat in the interests of clarity and brevity, but that is essentially how Paul saw — came to see — the matter.

For we can trace movement in his thought. "Start with ourselves," Paul says to Peter; "we are Jews, not sinners picked up out of the Gentile world. But does that make any difference, such as would justify our taking our supper in a different place from Titus, the Gentile? What is our basic conviction as Christians? It is faith in Jesus Christ. We put our faith in him in order that we might be justified by this faith in Jesus Christ, for no one is justified by works of law." The great words, *pistis, pisteuein, dikaioun, erga nomou* (faith, believe, justify, works of the law), all occur here, and it would take a long time to discuss them all seriously.

The important thing to note in a brief discussion is that though in this short paragraph Paul's thought spreads out far beyond the immediate situation it begins within that situation. It follows that works of law are, for example, the things that a Jew will do or abstain from doing in obedience to God when he sits at table to take a meal. The context of the epistle as a whole supplies circumcision as another representative work, or "thing done." "Works of law" (*erga nomou*) are the negative element, mentioned in verse 16 three times (*nomos*, "law," occurs another three times in this short paragraph); the corresponding positive term is the name *Christ*, mentioned eight times in verses 15–21 (twice in combination with Jesus). These are for Paul different ways by which people may think they can be rightly related to God (justified). The alternatives are twice starkly stated in verse 16, and the false alternative is excluded by a (mis)quotation of Psalm 143:3, *ex ergōn nomou ou dikaiōthēsetai pasa sarx* ("by works of law shall no flesh be justified.") The quotation is presumably made from memory; it is interesting that *pasa sarx* ("all flesh," instead of *pas zōn*, "every living person"), slips in to describe the inability of man to justify himself; *ex ergōn nomou* ("by works of the law") is there not only to suit the context but because the law, and works done in obedience to it, constitute the highest conceivable, though still inadequate, human claim.

Paul is arguing not merely that Gentiles are not to be obliged

to observe the rules of purity; it is wrong for Jews, who also are
justified by faith and not by works, to insist that such rules should
be observed in order that they may be able to join in a meal. It
is this, or a Jewish reaction to it, that underlies and explains the
protasis of verse 17: "If by seeking to be justified in Christ we ourselves also were found to be sinners. . . . " Seeking to be justified in
Christ without works of law will involve the Jews in sharing meals
with their Gentile Christian neighbors. This will make them, in the
technical sense, sinners. Does this mean that Christ becomes a min-
ister of sin, the effect of his action being to make us sinners? Paul
takes this thought into a different context: "No; if anyone makes
me a sinner I do it myself (*parabatēn emauton synistanō*). And I do
this (as Peter has done) when I build up again distinctions which
previously I had destroyed." All this results from the law, or rather
from the insistence that "We must have from Gentiles if not the
whole law at least part of the law, a token of the law. We Jews
must continue to observe it, and if we are to do so and also to
have fellowship with Gentiles, then the Gentiles must observe it
too, at least in part." To this Paul replies with the most absolute
of negatives. "The law? I am dead to it. I do not exist for it, and
it does not exist for me." This is emphatic and clear enough. But
Paul elucidates (though many would say that he obscures) his point
by adding two words: *dia nomou nomō apethanon* ("through law
I died to law"). What does "through law" mean?

Paul continues his statement with the words "I have been crucified [and this certainly means death] with Christ." Are "through
law" and "with Christ" to be regarded as synonymous? It does not
seem probable. Crucifixion with Christ is a death that has a positive outcome already hidden within it; sooner or later it will lead
to life with Christ. A parallel saying in Romans 7:4 is often ad-
duced: "You were put to death to the law (*ethanatōthēte tō nomō*)
through the body of Christ." This is itself a difficult saying. If it
means through the dead body of Christ, the dying of Christ, it is
a good parallel to the *Christō synestaurōmai* ("I have been crucified with Christ") of Galatians 2:19, but it does not explain *dia
nomou* ("through law"), though this is not to deny that there is
a connection between the death of Jesus and the law. In our passage Paul gives the goal of death to law as *hina theō zēsō* ("that
I may live to God"), suggesting that this dying is in his mind connected with the death and resurrection that are the beginning of the

Christian life. But we still have no explanation of "dying through law." There is in Romans a closer and more useful verse, 7:10: "The commandment that was intended to lead to life (*hē eis zōēn*) proved to be death (*eis thanaton*) for me." This, Paul explains, was not the law's fault; the fault was sin's fault, and sin was shown more clearly for what it is by the fact that it could so pervert and misuse that good, holy, and spiritual thing, the law. In Galatians also, though in a context determined by sin, death comes through the law. Here too, Paul defends the law. It is not in itself contrary to the promises of God, but it could not give life (3:21), and it served God's purpose only during the interlude between Moses and Christ.

Discussion of the problematical *dia nomou* ("through law") in 2:19 has deflected us from the main observation that comes to light in that verse, as verse 16 is taken up again. As long as we allow ourselves to be dominated by law and to work in the field determined and defined by law, we can do no better than reach compromises, which may at best provide temporary solutions for our problems but only at the risk of creating new ones. The only answer to the problems that the councils seek to solve is given in one word: Christ. The one name, the one person, is considered first subjectively, then objectively. Subjectively, Christ means for Paul his own death and resurrection. He has been crucified with Christ; there is now a new, risen life, which is not to be thought of as his own but as the life of Christ within him. He moves here on the edge of mysticism, and his words have often been taken to have a mystical meaning. They are, however, immediately and starkly interpreted by the word *flesh* and, in a different way, by the word *faith*. Paul's present life is in the flesh, lived in the context of, lived as part of, the ordinary world of material existence, circumscribed by both physical and moral considerations. And he does not live by sight, the vision of heavenly things, but by faith, trusting as Abraham did in a promise that is only a promise and not a possession. "Christ in me," like "I in Christ," is not mysticism but eschatology, an anticipation of the life that lies beyond death and resurrection and can be known only by faith.

With this we have already moved from the subjective to the objective. Faith is directed to a historical event, which is so stated as to be given thereby an immediate interpretation. "I have been crucified with Christ; he was crucified for me, manifesting his love and acting on my behalf." The full conclusion is drawn in verse 21. To do as Peter and Barnabas are doing, drawing distinctions and separating believer from believer by the application of dietary and purity laws, is to make void the grace of God, which is free and for all, a gift to be received, unfettered by legal provisions. This is not the way to secure a right relation with God; this is given by Christ crucified, and if it were achievable in any other way, Christ might as well not have died. Paul may have joined in the debating, compromising process for a while, but here he comes home to the fact that settles all arguments.

In Galatians 3 Paul resumes the argument in the context of Galatia rather than of Antioch. It had been important to set the record straight and in particular to show his amicable, though hardly deep, relation with the Jerusalem apostles and the Jerusalem church, a relation that persisted until they, represented by James, showed their dependence on legalism by attempting to force it on the Gentile element in the church of Antioch. Paul now goes on to take up scriptural arguments, some at least of which his adversaries had used — probably in Galatia but no doubt also elsewhere. The material is set out so as to tell the story of God's dealings with his people; these reach a climax at the end of the chapter and in the first verses of chapter 4.

The story begins with Abraham, with whom God entered into a covenant. This was based on faith, the ground on which Abraham was accounted righteous. "Abraham believed God, and it was counted to him as righteousness" (3:6). This means that not race determines a relation with God, but faith. Moreover, it was specifically stated that the Gentiles were to be included in the process. God announced the good news, the gospel, in advance: "In you shall all the Gentiles be blessed" — and *as* Gentiles, that is, as those who depend solely on faith. The corollary of this follows and is expressed in biblical language. Those who depend on works of law, trusting in their legal achievements, receive not a blessing but a curse. This is the curse promised for all those who do not abide in all the provisions of the law. That no one does abide in all the things that are written in the law is proved by another Old Testament verse: "It is those who are righteous by faith who shall live" (3:11). Here Paul pulls up for a moment: Does not this mean that all will be cursed, none blessed? Who has done the whole law? No, this is not the consequence, for the sinless Christ, who was hanged on a tree, has taken the curse for us, so that we are free. This is how the cross comes to mean righteousness for those who in faith accept it. The end of the story is now anticipated. The promise was made to Abraham and his seed. That might seem to mean not to the Gentiles but only to the Israelites, Abraham's descendants. No, says Paul, the word *seed* is singular, *spermati,* not *spermasi.* Thus the climax of the story lies not with ethnic Israel but with Christ, and (in Christ) his people.

But Paul has been going too fast. Verse 17 is most clearly understood as a reply to an opponent who makes the point, "Yes, this may be all very well as far as Abraham and God's covenant with Abraham are concerned. But after Abraham came the even greater figure of Moses, and the basis of the covenant is changed. It is no longer a matter of promise and faith but of law and works. Only those who perform the works that the law requires will now inherit." To this Paul answers, playing on the word *diathēkē,* which means both "covenant" and "testament": "When a testator has sealed his will, no one can alter it; the law was given 430 years after the covenant and cannot change it." A reply comes back, "There is one person who can change a testament; the testator." But Paul still has a shot in his locker. "The law was not given directly by God (who made the covenant), but by angels." The covenant of promise and faith still stands.

Paul's interlocutor now has a question. "If the law cannot change things, what is it for? Why was it given?" A good question. The answer is that the law is not to be thought of as a bad thing. It is not itself the conveyer of promise, but it is not against God's promises. It comes through angels but from the same gracious God and is itself a gift of grace. But the covenant of law was a covenant of obedience (Exod. 19:5, 8; 24:3, 7–8), and the law was a temporary measure. From 3:19 to the end of the chapter the text is full of temporal clauses: "might be given," "before faith came," "till faith should be revealed," "up to the time of Christ," "now that faith has come," "no longer." These all emphasize the temporary character of the law. It was not there at the beginning of the process, and it will not be there at the end. It has therefore not altered the fundamental character of the original covenant, which on the human side is not secured by works of law but is received by faith. The law, in addition to providing valid guidance for the conduct of life, had the effect of imprisoning humankind — of imprisoning the whole universe, if we are to give full weight to the neuter *ta panta* ("everything") in verse 22 — under the sovereignty of sin.

The thought is taken up again in verse 24, where the image of the *paidagōgos* is used. The *paidagōgos* is not a teacher who will in due course lead to the supreme teacher, but the slave who will prevent the schoolboy from playing truant. As long as the law ruled, where the law ruled, there was no escape from the dominion of sin, until the possibility of faith in Christ came into being. Once faith came on the scene the *paidagōgos* was gone. Looking back through chapter 3 we may well ask what had become of faith since the time of Abraham. It is a question Paul does not ask; not surprisingly there is no answer. If Paul meant that faith was banished by the law he was being unfair both to the law and to many who lived under it. The question arises again at the end of Romans 9 and the beginning of 10. Notwithstanding Israel's zeal for God they had misunderstood the law, thinking that it asked for nothing but works and not perceiving that the true response to it was faith. The recognition of this truth about the law marks not a contradiction of Galatians but an advance, in that it answers a question that in Galatians was not asked.

The climax of the chapter, which may be regarded as the climax (within the epistle) of Paul's rejection of the temporizing compromise and legalism of Jerusalem, comes in 3:26–29. Faith means being in Christ Jesus. You were baptized into Christ, you put on Christ, you belong to Christ. It makes no difference whether you are Jew or Greek, slave or free, male or female; he is the seed of Abraham, heir of the promise, and those who are in him receive in him their share of the promise, themselves the seed of Abraham, that is, the people of God.

We may note briefly that Paul continues for another paragraph, probably because he remembers that he is writing for Gentiles who, though they seem to be taking up the Jewish law, began their lives outside it. This does not mean that they escape bondage, though bondage under the law has been replaced by bondage under the cosmic powers (*stoicheia tou kosmou*). Paul uses a new image, that of the heir, who is the rightful owner of the whole estate but, as long as he is a minor, is no better off than a slave. The end of the story is the same: "when the fullness of time came God sent forth his Son to redeem" — and he still says "those who were under the law," for indeed all humankind, not only Jews, owe obedience to their Creator. There is an important parallel between 3:29 and 4:9. It is the same person, now presented for the benefit of Gentile readers not as Christ, the fulfillment of Judaism, but as the Son of God, who makes compromise impossible and himself constitutes the alternative to compromise. One does not ask, "Can we give a little here and gain a little there?" One asks, "What does it mean to have Christ the Son of God as Lord and Redeemer?" When the question is so put there is no doubt what the answer will be.

This is, I think, the clearest example in Paul of the way in which a more commonplace argument is replaced, or hammered home, by an emphatic christological assertion. It is clear because here Paul begins by quoting what he said to Peter and continues either with his second thoughts on the occasion itself or with his subsequent more mature thought. Elsewhere in the epistles we have, as one would expect, the argument as Paul, having thought the matter over, decided it should go. There are, however, other examples of this change of approach; there is a notable one in 1 Corinthians 11, in which Paul deals with the disgraceful behavior of the Corinthians at the church supper, for which at this time we have no reason to presuppose an established eucharistic liturgy, or indeed a Eucharist. In 11:17–22 Paul berates his readers as one might any society holding an accustomed supper party and behaving badly. "One is hungry, another gets drunk. Haven't you houses for eating and drinking?" But then (vv. 23–26), "Remember the Lord Jesus at his supper party.... You proclaim the Lord's death until he comes. How can you do that and mock your poor hungry brother?"

Another notable example is found in Philippians 2, modified by the fact that the first verse of the chapter contains already a reference to Christ; after that, however, Paul appeals to the Philippian community for unity on the secular ground that it will give him pleasure: "Complete my joy by having the same mind, the same love, united in soul." Immediately after this follows the christological passage: "Who, though he existed in the form of God, thought life on equality with God no prize worth keeping, but humbled himself, took the form of a slave...." Commonplace exhortations to humility are nothing in comparison with this account of the Lord's humiliation.

These are outstanding examples of the way in which Paul will sidestep, or sometimes sweep aside, other arguments and considerations in order to concentrate on the figure of Christ. This becomes explicit in the most vital of contexts when he declares, with reference to his first preaching in Corinth, "I decided to know nothing among you except Jesus Christ, and him crucified" (1 Cor. 2:2). No doubt this would include the addition made in the words of Romans 8:34, "Christ Jesus who died, or rather was raised, who is at the right hand of God, who makes intercession for us." The whole is summed up in the formula "the word of faith," which is a preaching rather than a baptismal formula, though it would serve both purposes. "If you confess with your mouth Jesus as Lord, and believe in your heart that God raised him from the dead, you will be saved" (Rom. 10:9). These were propositions on which, for Paul, no compromise was possible; conversely, agreement on these made agreement with others (pillars, superapostles) possible.

Even here, however, if my reconstruction of the controversies of the apostolic age is correct, Paul learned the hard way that compromise did not work. It would have worked to say, Jesus is the Jewish Messiah. He himself worked among Jews; he fulfilled the Jewish Bible, his message is for Jews, and what God has done through him he has done for his own people. If others are to join them and share with them in the blessings of the messianic age they must first become Jews in the manner laid down long ago and consistently practiced. I say, "It would have worked." It would have produced a united community. It would not have worked very well; not many converts would have been made. The church, though it would not have borne that name, would have been a subset of Pharisaism. The name of Jesus would today be no better known than that of Sabbatai Zevi, the seventeenth-century messiah.

It did work, as we know, to throw the barriers down, proclaiming Christ as the sole and all-sufficient author of salvation, a salvation free and accessible to all, whether Jews or Gentiles. But the account of the council in Galatians 2 seems to present the Jerusalem pillars as saying: "Very well, you may understand the gospel in that way and take it to the Gentiles; we agree that your converts need not be circumcised; they will be the Gentile, uncircumcised, part of the people of God. We for our part will go our own way, preaching to Jews and accepting only those Gentiles who are willing to become Jews." That this did not work appeared speedily in Antioch. James in the interests of Judaism called for and obtained a separation into two churches that could not sit together at table and eat in fellowship the same food. So much for the right hand of fellowship in Jerusalem. Peter and Paul, who had shaken hands in Jerusalem, could only oppose each other in Antioch. Paul — at that time or after later reflection — found his way to the solution of the problem. There was no way but by a reference to the one first principle. "We agree on the preaching of Christ crucified and risen; if righteousness comes through the law this proclamation is a waste of time and its content is a wasted life. Christ need not have died. Since this is absurd we must conclude that he is our righteousness and that, as a means of achieving righteousness, we are dead to the law and the law is dead to us."

It was not this conclusion that was reached in a new council at Jerusalem but a new compromise. And it must be admitted that this compromise worked. The decree produced by the council (Acts 15:29) proposed a basic Judaism, which Gentile sympathizers with Judaism probably already kept. For them the decree asked nothing fresh, and they would have no difficulty, either in theology or in practice, in accepting it. It has been maintained that it was these sympathizers, already to be found in the synagogue, that Paul for the most part addressed, and that it was among them that his Gentile converts were found. This seems doubtful. The Gentile Christians in Thessalonica had turned to the living and true God from idols (1 Thess. 1:9); this could not be said of men who regularly attended the synagogue. The converts in Corinth included (1 Cor. 6:9–11) fornicators, idolaters, adulterers, catamites, sodomites, thieves, the rapacious, drunkards, revilers, robbers; this does not sound like a synagogue congregation. 1 Corinthians 12:2 speaks explicitly of a past in which Corinthians were driven to dumb idols. The vices listed in Gal. 5:19–21 were probably not unknown to the Galatians. It seems, however, that as Christians these Gentiles also were prepared to accept much of Judaism, and the decree was taken (by Luke, for example) as the basis of the Gentile mission, which all eventually accepted; and it was observed for centuries. It demanded the bare minimum of Jewish custom and rule; even so, the rules were often bent.

I have referred earlier to the version of the decree found in Revelation 2, and to the Western text of Acts 15:20, 29; 21:25. This means that many churches understood the decree to have required no more than abstention from idolatry and fornication, together with a general Christian kindliness. To this no one would object, certainly not Paul. The Western variants, however, remain variations from Luke's understanding of the decree; and it must be remembered that Acts 15 is fundamentally concerned not with the question "With whom may I have supper and what shall we eat?" but "Who may be saved and on what conditions?" Circumcision is excluded from the conditions, probably not because it was one outstanding piece of legalism but because it was so repulsive to the Greco-Roman mind that to insist on it would have prevented the spread of Christianity into the Greco-Roman world. The conditions included not circumcision, but elements of Jewish law taken for the most part from its ethical provisions.

Luke in Acts, written probably in the 80s, presents to us the basis on which the church was organized and its mission conducted in the immediately postapostolic period. So Paul lost, and the Stephen party, with its via media and its Gentile base in the synagogue fringe, won. The church owed, and Luke at least knew that it owed, not only its establishment in a substantial part of the Roman Empire but also its independence of Judaism, and therewith its universal scope, to Paul. The author, or authors, of the Pastoral Epistles knew this too, and for them Paul was the apostle par excellence, a step that even Luke does not take. But they like Luke fail to state with unambiguous clarity Paul's radical gospel of radically unconditional grace. The message was based on a compromise, and so was Christian society.

So what are we to say about the theology of the council, of the postapostolic age? If you will, of Acts? The period was one in which the Gentile element in the church was increasing; but Jacob Jervell has argued, not without force, that the Jewish Christian minority exercised a surprising and disproportionate influence, putting the decree into circulation and observance, maintaining the Matthean element in the gospel tradition, and, in its early stages, affecting Paul himself to the extent of drawing from him the discussion in Romans 9–11 of the ultimate destiny of Israel. It is better, however, to see these things, at least the decree and the influence of the Jewish Christian party, as arising from the Jews of the Diaspora who were at home in the Hellenistic world. These forces had permeated Luke's mind to such an extent that he told the story of his hero Paul in terms of them. He could even make Paul a member and an agent of the decree-making body, and attribute to him the Areopagus speech of Acts 17.

For the most part it will suffice to say that Luke was a less profound theologian than Paul; if this is a sin it affects us all, and none of us can afford to throw stones at Luke's glass house. Again and again Luke stops short of the point Paul had reached a generation earlier. It is so for example in christology. Luke can write in Acts 2:36 a sentence that, taken on its own, appears to mean that the man Jesus became Lord and Christ when God vindicated him after his crucifixion. That Luke himself believed that Jesus was Christ and Lord from his birth is shown by Luke 2:11. Did Luke himself not see the difference? Did he think it unimportant? There can be no doubt of Luke's personal loyalty to Jesus, but he had not grasped the fact that a serious christology, an absolute loyalty, demands something like preexistence. This is to be seen with special clarity in passages such as Philippians 2:6–11, where Paul appears to modify less well thought-out christologies. Luke, one supposes, would have been quite satisfied with the Philippians' hymn before Paul edited it.

Again, there is in Acts virtually no doctrine of the atonement. One verse is always pointed out as the exception to this theological silence — Acts 20:28. The exception is important, but it is not followed up, and Luke's word (*peripoieisthai,* "obtain") has no other theological use in the New Testament. Elsewhere Luke is content to say little more than that the crucifixion was a bad thing — a mistake, even a sin — but one that God put right by means of the resurrection. It goes with this that Luke is fully aware of Christian baptism, baptism into the name of Jesus, but does not think of it as specifically baptism into Christ's death; he knows that Christians meet to break bread, that is, to have a meal together, but he does not find it necessary to say that at their meal they proclaim the Lord's death with a view to his future coming. All this, however, is a matter of omission, and omission does not necessarily mean disagreement. Acts is a vindication of the Christianity of the ordinary person in the pew: see how well you can do without a great deal of theology!

But there are vital points at which you cannot do without theology; one (and it has arisen more than once in the history of the church) is the confrontation of law with grace and faith. If to be saved it is necessary to abstain from food sacrificed to idols, can we believe that Paul was saved? Such a question reduces the matter to absurdity; but that in turn underlines the importance in theology of saying exactly what you mean and not using compromise for-

mulas that can be interpreted in more ways than one or attempting
to let everyone have at least a bit of his own way. "To become as a
Jew to the Jews" is good as a matter of social courtesy; as a way of
salvation such occasional obedience would be worse than no obedience at all. The church on the whole accepted the decree and the
church did not disintegrate, but it did turn into something more
like an institution and less like a family.

Two things, however, secured the persistence of Christianity.
One was the adaptability of the decree. With some textual vari-
ation, or even without that expedient, it could be reduced to an
elementary moral code that rejected idolatry and so maintained
faithfulness to the one God of Scripture and regarded fornication
and bloodshed as evil. The other was the faithfulness of all parties,
including the heirs of James and of Stephen, to the one gospel of
Christ crucified and risen, ultimately incompatible as it was with
any form of legalism. To these may be added the lasting influence
of Paul. He may have been imperfectly represented in Acts, in the
Pastorals, in 1 Clement and Ignatius, but even untheological hero-
worship helped to preserve the letters, with their power to revive
and reform the church. And with these we must count the influence of the only indirectly Pauline, but no less profound, theology
of the Fourth Gospel.

Conclusion
Discussion
and
Implications

The discussion sparked by the lectures of Professors Hengel and Barrett was exciting and informative. This was due in no small measure to the panels of respondents identified in the introduction. I can here give only some of the main points that were raised by the respondents and from the floor together with a sense of the exchange that took place on these two occasions. I will add some concluding thoughts concerning the implications of these lectures and discussion for the future.

What follows is by no means a transcript of the discussion, although it often makes use of the exact words spoken. I have often abbreviated and condensed the discussion, and I have taken the liberty to reorder the material freely so that related topics could be brought together.

Discussion with Professor Hengel

All the panelists expressed substantial and enthusiastic agreement with the main theses put forward by Hengel. I should indicate that they responded only to the first main section of his essay together with the concluding points at the end of the essay.

1. Hengel's central affirmation that Christianity took root from Jewish soil found strong and unanimous support among the panelists. But as Hengel anticipates in the second paragraph of his

essay, his insistence that it grew *entirely* out of Judaism proved problematic for several of the panel members. Such a conclusion would entail, according to Hengel's second point, that Hellenistic elements of the New Testament were mediated entirely via Hellenistic Judaism rather than being drawn directly from pagan Hellenistic thought.

Ralph Martin pointed to the importance of Hengel's thesis given the repeated claims that Paul was directly dependent upon pagan religious thought, for example, in the improbable suggestion that Paul would have acquired knowledge of pagan religions in his hometown of Tarsus. While agreeing with Hengel's point, he raised the question whether in some places the New Testament might nevertheless indicate direct Hellenistic influence. Martin wondered, for example, about gnosis at Corinth and whether the various problems Paul encountered there might have any connection with some form of proto-Gnosticism. Could this have influenced the language used by Paul in the Corinthian correspondence? Martin also indicated that the more marginal books of the New Testament raise the question even more sharply. For example, does the language of 2 Peter 1:4 about making humans divine (i.e., "partakers of the divine nature," *theias koinōnoi physeōs*) come from a Jewish notion of *theopoiēsis* ("deification") or from pagan thought?

Playing off Hengel's quotation of Fergus Millar ("The world of the gospels is that of Josephus"), David Scholer noted that although Josephus was born from the womb of Judaism, when he wrote his literature he flirted with Greco-Roman thinking and in some cases expressed Jewish ideas in Greco-Roman ideology that was not mediated through Hellenistic Judaism but was a part of either his apologetic intent or his way of understanding in the later period of his life. Scholer suggested that the situation may be similar when we come to the authors of the New Testament. Although all the primal origins of the church are to be located in Judaism, even in the New Testament the authors began to dress the new Jewish baby in Greco-Roman clothes. An example of a Cynic-Stoic concept in the New Testament that may have been unmediated through Hellenistic Judaism, Scholer pointed out, might be Paul's use of *autarkēs* in Philippians 4:11 (cf. *autarkeia* in 1 Tim. 6:6), where Paul talks about the "contentment" he knows "in any and all circumstances." He further mentioned the problem of the "spiritual body" in 1 Corinthians 15, and he also wondered whether the

Pauline emphasis on celibacy was derived totally from Hellenistic Judaism.

Hengel's response. Of course Josephus had learned from the pagans in the same way as other Jews had. He had been a colleague and opponent of Justus of Tiberias, and they both attended the Greek school to learn rhetoric. He occasionally uses the word *tychē* ("fortune") in the *Jewish War* because he is writing to Roman readers. Nevertheless he does not believe in the Greek goddess Tyche, and his use of the word does not change his Judaism. His Jewish identity, strong from the beginning, only gets stronger. It is correct that the Jewish authors of the New Testament can clothe their ideas in Greco-Roman cloth, but I would say this cloth already comes from a Jewish tailor. For many years there had been hundreds of synagogues from the Syrian border to Spain holding their services in the Greek language. These Jewish presbyters and scribes read literature in the Greek language, and they forged their biblical ethics employing Stoic and Platonic vocabulary. Most remarkable is the translation of the Septuagint beginning in the third century B.C., where we can see Greco-Roman cloth being taken over by the Jews. And it was already seen to fit the Jewish faith well. They translated the self definition of God before Moses in Exodus 3:14, "I will be" or "I am who I am," in a Greek philosophical, Platonic way: *egō eimi ho ōn*, "I am 'the being' " — God's being. You see, this is a Jew taking Greco-Roman cloth, cloth that fits well and which can be used to tell his truth. This is important.

We cannot prove that one sentence in the New Testament was taken directly from a pagan author or pagan thinker rather than being mediated through the Jewish Hellenistic background of the authors. The simple reason for this is that the Jews had already taken over so much material and thought from the Greeks and Romans. Nevertheless, these Jews did not become syncretistic in so doing. They did not change their proper faith in the one God and his law or in their belief that they were the chosen people of God. No, they became even stronger in their identity. Within this rich Jewish-Hellenistic milieu, spread throughout the Roman Empire at that time, early Christianity grew. So we cannot prove that there was a direct influence of pagan thought upon the writers of the New Testament. Of course Paul did not learn paganism in Tarsus. But he learned his Hellenistic language, Hellenistic terms like *physis* ("nature") or *syneidēsis* ("conscience") by means of the Greek-speaking synagogue because, as Philo says, the synagogue is the school of the true philosophy. And our philosophy is better and older than that of Plato and Aristotle, because they have learned from us. I think that when a Jew took up the *Timaeus* of Plato and read of the *dēmiourgos*, the Demiurge, who created the world, he must have thought that here was a Greek author who had read Moses. He would have believed that the Greeks took over Jewish ideas and used them for their own purposes.

It is necessary to allow for the possibility that Christianity may itself have produced some innovative ideas, something new over against both Judaism and the pagan world. Perhaps, for example, the *sōma christou*, the "body of Christ," as a spiritual entity has no real parallel. You do have in Jewish mysticism, in the *Shiʿur Qomah*, reference to the immense frame of the body of God. And if we think of the Ancient of Days in Daniel 7 as having a body of fire, this is in some way a preparation for the spiritual body, because spirit is fire. There is, however, no need here for direct pagan influence.

The word *autarkeia* comes from Stoic philosophy, but Philo likes it very much too. For him the ideal, wise person must be *autarkēs*. This view finds antecedents in the Jewish wisdom literature. The synagogues in Greek-speaking countries would also have referred to "self-sufficiency" as an important virtue.

To a question from the floor along similar lines, Hengel added the following remarks. My argument is not a theological one; it is a historical one. It is not my opinion of salvation history that there could not be any syncretistic or pagan influence. I simply do not know a place where we can confidently say that this is direct influence from pagan authors. From the evidence of the sources, the first evidence of direct dependence upon pagan language is found in Ignatius, when he speaks of the Eucharist as the *pharmakon athanasias*, "medicine of immortality" (Ign. *Eph*. 20.2). Here we have no Jewish parallel, whereas we do find the language in the Isis cult. As far as I see, however, much of this mystery language is found already in Wisdom and Philo. And this is true much more than in the New Testament. It is strange that the language of the New Testament is much less Hellenistic than is the language of the Jewish Hellenistic writers.

The following question was also put from the floor. Although the separation of Judaism and Christianity came later, the Gentile mission did come at a very early stage. Is this not a historical point to be taken into consideration because it opens the door to Hellenistic influence on early Christianity? Professor Hengel responded as follows. Judaism had been under Hellenistic influence for four hundred years, even in Palestine. With this we may compare the mere seventy years of earliest Christianity in the New Testament period. Of course it could be said that these God-fearers or Gentiles who became Christians must have brought their beliefs with them. But when we see the influence of their past beliefs upon their conduct, as we do in Corinth, when, for example, they went into the pagan temples for dinners and so forth, Paul is adamant in his opposition to them. More than the liberal Jews of the Diaspora, Paul resisted any such compromise. I think he is even more strictly against all sorts of polytheism.

2. Ralph Martin noted the question of the Christians' self-identity in the New Testament period as still a matter for open discussion. It seems clear that we are not to think of early Christians as simply reformed Jews or messianic Jews. This would seem to underestimate the degree of newness and discontinuity they reflect. What are we to make of that piece of christology in Acts 3:20–21, which refers to Jesus as the Messiah who is appointed to come, a kind of *messias futurus* or *messias designatus,* and evidently not the Messiah in reality? Is J. A. T. Robinson correct to call this the earliest christology of all? Are we to think of this as an erratic block, a foreign body? According to Ernst Käsemann, early Christianity should not be thought of as a revamped Judaism. What is it then? It obviously entails fulfillment of the old covenant.

But this brings us to a further question. If the central elements of Second Temple Judaism in the first century are understandings of temple and Torah, can early Christianity simply be described as new understandings of these realities — a new, eschatological temple and the displacement of Torah by the Messiah, a Messiah contra Torah, as Hengel puts it? A description such as this, however, leaves us with a body of material that cannot be enclosed in those categories — for example, the "new creation" (*kainē ktisis*) of 2 Corinthians 5:17, or the reference in Ephesians 2:15 to the purpose of God in Christ to create "one new person" (*heis kainos anthrōpos*). This new reality is neither Jewish nor Christian but a new creation or a third race if you will, as in Aristides or the apologists. Is there not a trace of that in Paul, who in 1 Corinthians 10:32 can write "Give no offense to Jews or to Greeks or to the church of God." Is this where the concept of a "third race" originates?

Scholer called attention to 1 Corinthians 10:31–32 and its importance to the question of the partings of the ways. Here Paul summarizes his argument from 8:1 on, about eating meat offered to idols, and now he generalizes about how the Corinthians ought to behave and that they should not give offense to any of the three groups, the Jews, the Greeks, or the church of God. According to Scholer, this threefold division is a flag indicating not that Paul here announces a Christian self-identity such as seems to emerge in the second century, in Ignatius, but that Paul is teetering on the edge of an understanding of the movement we call the church as something distinct and separate from Judaism. This raises some questions for understanding the parting of the ways.

Hengel's response. First Corinthians 10:31–32 points not to a third people, a *triton genos,* but refers to the true Israel, the eschatological people of God that will soon receive its returning Lord. It is not a new religion. This is the view from outside, perhaps a philosophical view in the Hegelian sense, or as with F. C. Baur and E. P. Sanders, the different patterns of Christianity and Judaism. But Paul did not think of Christianity as a new, distinct religion, and a new group between Greeks and Jews. He thinks instead that the church is "the Israel of God" (Gal. 6:16). The church is the eschatological people, the *ekklēsia,* which means the *qahal adonai,* the "church of the Lord," the eschatological assembly of God awaiting the coming Lord. This is a definite difference. Speaking about Jews and Greeks, the New Testament makes a difference between the ethnic name "the Jews" — that is, ethnic, political *Ioudaioi* — and Israel, which is the holy name of salvation history.

The word *ekklēsia* is drawn from the Septuagint, where it translates mainly *qahal* but sometimes *edah,* which is usually translated *synagogē.* With their eschatological consciousness, the Christians, as early as the Hellenists, deliberately chose this word *ekklēsia,* in an eschatological sense, as referring to the last true people of God. But it remains important that all Israel will enter this people of

God with the coming of Christ, according to Romans 11, even if now they disbelieve. This is quite another development than we find in the second and third century with the term "third people" or *triton genos*.

On the question of the new creation, it is interesting that we have this term *beriyah hadasha*, "the new creation," in the Qumran scrolls. That community thought and felt themselves to be the *beriyah hadasha*, the one true, eschatological people of God. Here is a close parallel to early Christian consciousness. Because the old *beriyah* is sinful and corrupt, it must be renewed by the eschatological miracle of the new creation of God. And here too at Qumran we have the term the *kabod adam*, "the glory of Adam." The same thing is in view in the reference to falling short of the glory of God (*doxa tou theou*) in Romans 3:23. This is the glory that Adam had in paradise, and the same thing is in view in Paul's reference to Christ as the last Adam (1 Cor. 15:45) as the one who brings back the lost glory of God and recreates the new world of God at the end of time.

As for the christology of Acts 3:20–21, I don't accept the view of F. Hahn and others that the resurrected one is only the Messiah designate. He is, on the contrary, the elevated Messiah who sits at the right hand of God, and therefore he already bears the title *mashiach* in a way not true before his passion. He now sits at the right hand of God, almost in unity with God himself, and from there he will come again. The resurrection was nearly from the beginning understood not as Jesus being hidden somewhere in heaven but as elevated to the right hand of God as the last revealer of God's salvation. Psalm 110 was used very early in the Christian community to interpret Christ as the cursed and crucified Messiah now elevated to sit on the throne at the right hand of God. Thus being elevated, he is the Lord. The title *lord, adonai* (Greek *kyrios*), applied to Jesus, comes especially from the earliest Christian use of Psalm 110, "The Lord said to my lord."

The question was put from the floor concerning whether Galatians 1:13–14 did not mean that Judaism was something of the past for Paul. Hengel responded by saying that *en tō Ioudaïsmō* means not the Jewish people but learning of the law, being a Pharisee. As a young Pharisee scholar Paul was like a fervent theological student studying the center of Christian theology. When

Paul uses the verb *proekopton,* this is typical Stoic vocabulary. But the success he refers to is in the learning of the law.

3. Seyoon Kim raised the question of how the earliest Christians overcame the Jewish particularism associated with election and were able to move eventually to a consciousness of their faith as a universal movement. Should we not, he asked, accept the argument of Paul and other Christians that in the Christ event God fulfilled his promise to Abraham to bless all the nations through the seed of Abraham, or the argument that in the Christ event God revealed the goal of his election of Israel, namely, to make it a light to the nations? So, for example, in Galatians 3:23–4:7 Paul speaks of God sending his Son as the seed of Abraham so that by faith in him we become children of God — regardless of whether we are Jews or Gentiles — calling God *Abba,* Father. And in Romans 15:8–9 Christ became a servant of the Jews, the circumcision, in order to show God's faithfulness or truthfulness, that is, to confirm God's promises to the patriarchs, Abraham, Isaac, and Jacob, to bless the nations through the seed of Abraham. Thus it is through Israel that all the Gentiles may convert to and glorify the true and living God. So early Christianity became a universal movement because it understood the essence of the Old Testament revelation better than its Jewish guardians, who erected the Torah as the dividing wall, the fence or hedge, that protected the identity of Israel. In other words, in overcoming Jewish particularism the early Christians could understand themselves as being faithful to God's revelation in the Scriptures, as being more faithful to God's revelation than the unbelieving majority of the Jews who were preoccupied with the Torah as the dividing wall between themselves and the Gentiles. With this in mind, we can understand the early Christians' claim to be the true Israel over against the Jews.

Hengel's response. On the question of the universality implicit in election of Abraham I am in full agreement. There are several lines or possibilities in the Old Testament. One way went over the Torah to the rabbis; the other went over the promises and the prophets to the Christians. Both are understandable. To be noted about the promise to Abraham that "in you all the nations will be blessed" is that faith becomes an important element, as Genesis 15:6 shows.

This is fundamentally important. It is by faith — a faith like Abraham's — therefore, that Christians become themselves the seed of Abraham.

4. Scholer called attention to the impact of the Holocaust on Jewish-Christian dialogue and the agenda of New Testament scholarship today. In his view, an important contribution of Hengel's paper is its fostering of an understanding of the relationship between the church and Judaism. He expressed great appreciation of the section on anti-Judaism in New Testament, agreeing with Hengel that the New Testament is not anti-Semitic. For Scholer, two of the most troublesome texts in the New Testament, however, are Revelation 2:9 and 3:9, and he regards these texts as constituting one of the most difficult questions in our canon in terms of the parting of the ways.

Kim noted Hengel's comment that in this post-Holocaust era we should engage in dialogue with representatives of Judaism and we should state our respective positions unashamedly while respecting one another with full rights, and further that dialogue in this spirit will enable us to see not only the truth of our position but also truth of our sister religion. At the same time, Hengel made mention of how the New Testament Christians, especially Paul, stated the basic issue between Judaism and Christianity in terms of Christ and Torah, indeed, Christ *or* Torah. This remains the basic issue: whether redemption is through Christ or through the Torah, the Mosaic covenant. Here we have an either/or, or can there be a both/and? Martin reminded us that the parting of the ways between Christians and Jews — the division of early Christianity from Judaism — in the first century is an issue being debated vigorously among New Testament scholars. He stressed that the growth of Christianity from Jewish soil is important to note because it means that any debate between early Christians and Jews was strictly intramural. Martin further called attention to the lifting up of mutual learning and enrichment between Jews and Christians currently taking place, which will grow as Christian scholars and Jewish scholars maintain dialogue and do not oppose one another in an adversarial relationship. There is much to thank God for in the open and active discussion between Jews and Christians on a friendly basis and the decrease of a "them and us" attitude.

Hengel's response. In dialogue it is absolutely necessary that we have respect for our dialogue partners, even when we cannot wholly agree with them. This mutual respect is fundamentally important. And I must confess that after much encounter with Jews, pious and secular, I have a deep respect for all of them and also for their personal opinions. I am, nevertheless, a Christian believer, and for this reason Romans 9–11 is so important for me. The last word about Israel, as for us, will be spoken by God himself, the God of the Trinity, Father, Son and Spirit. A proper sincerity should be accompanied by a great openness to learning from Jews to understand our New Testament better. This seems to me very important. This anti-Jewish disposition on the part of Christians for centuries — which we should study — was a shame. It is not Christian. It made us Christians poorer. We sinned against our own faith. Being quite sure of the promises of God, we can be very open and respectful. We should as Christians love our Jewish brethren.

To a question from the floor about whether the Jews should be evangelized, Hengel responded as follows. Christians are sent to everybody, and in the New Testament the gospel is especially sent to the Jews. The apostles are sent to their own people. It is especially difficult for a German to give an answer to this question. I would say for myself, being a German, that I do not have this commission to evangelize the Jews. But the truth of the gospel is unquestionably a message given to Israel. Jesus was a Jew. The gospel is also for the Jews today. It would be anti-Christian and anti-Semitic to say now that the gospel is not for the Jews. But this evangelism must be done with toleration, with respect, with openness, and without any force or violence. We must be those who speak the truth in love (*alētheuontes en agapē*, Eph. 4:15).

Discussion with Professor Barrett

The panelists were in broad agreement with Professor Barrett's lecture, notwithstanding the fact that only one of the three, Walter Hansen, shares the view that Acts 15 and Galatians 2 refer to the same event. This issue, however, was put to the side, and the discussion proceeded with the assumption that the two passages describe the same event.

1. Ralph Martin began by recalling the illustration used by G. B. Caird about the New Testament witnesses as participants at a round-table discussion. In Acts 15 and Galatians 2 we encounter participants in such a dialogue. Our task is to listen to the voices of the various contributors, Paul, Peter, James. The problem is that our sources do not record everything that was said on the occasion of the council. If Paul was present at the council, as Acts 15 indicates, not a great deal of his mind is revealed to us. If he was not present at the council, then what might he have said had he been there? Perhaps the answer is that he would have said what he did say in the letter to the Galatians.

Barrett's response. It is a most interesting question to ask what Paul would have said had he been at the council. This grows more complicated as you think of the possibility of two councils, one at which the Gentile mission was discussed and one at which food laws were discussed. One can only imagine Paul contending earnestly for freedom to take the gospel into the Gentile world and equally objecting to any attempt to constrain Gentiles by the ceremonial laws of Judaism, for example, the dietary laws.

Why, asked Martin, was the decree of Acts 15 defective? According to Barrett, one of the omissions in the Jerusalem resolution was that it left out the central figure, who is Christ. Agreed, but why was the central issue, circumcision, left out? There are references to "those of the circumcision" in the prelude to the coming together of the council. But in terms of what they resolve and agree, circumcision is notably absent. The issues are dietary or food laws. From what we know of how those dietary laws functioned, they were ways by which people stayed in the community. They were identity markers for Judaism, and they were concerned with how people are to stay within the new community. They were to stay in by observing these abstentions. What the council was ostensibly concerned with, however, was how people get in. The distinction between getting in and staying in is important. Paul was more interested in how Gentiles get saved. James, it appears, speaks to the issue of how Gentiles stay in fellowship with their Jewish brothers and sisters.

Barrett's response. It is interesting to bring in the matter of the relation between staying in and getting in. One remembers that in the Acts account the whole matter arises out of the demand made in Antioch by people who come from Judea insisting that Gentiles get into the Christian faith only by way of circumcision: "It is necessary to circumcise them" (Acts 15:5). Circumcision is essentially a "getting in" business — getting into the people of God who have had this regulation given to them, that male members of the people should be circumcised on the eighth day if they are born into a Jewish family or on conversion if they are not. So that there is a strong getting in element in the context of the Acts account of the council. I think that part of our difficulty is that both of these questions are relevant and must have been discussed at some point. It has often been maintained — I do not think it is true, but I can understand the view — that Luke's account in Acts 15 shifts as it goes along. It starts with a question: Does a Gentile convert have to be circumcised? And that is a getting in question. Some people say that the council finishes up with what is a "staying in" question: How are Gentile Christians and Jewish Christians to be able to eat together? I do not think that is so. As I see it, in Acts 15:19 James speaks about the necessity of his rules. That is to say, it is not just a matter of how Gentiles may accommodate themselves to Jews when both are in. It is still a question of what you have got to do to be a Christian if you are a Gentile. So I think that the question of staying in is lurking there in the background. It boils over in Antioch in Galatians 2:11. But it had not been fully settled previously. And I think that it is then that the decree comes in. So that one has a complicated story here that includes both elements — getting in and staying in.

To Barrett's statement that compromise never works, Martin added the following. If people take a stand against compromise, as Paul did, it is a costly business. And Paul paid a heavy price for it. Yet at the same time it was productive. Paul never uses the decree, he never refers to it, when he might have — for example, at Corinth. Paul's stand against the decree alienated him from the pillar apostles, from Barnabas, and from Antioch. The results of this refusal to compromise are the following. Negatively, it isolated Paul and it alienated him from his home base at Antioch. On the positive side, however, the fruitfulness of his refusal to compromise was that it gave a new definition to his understanding of justification by faith alone. It clarified the sense in which Christ was the central element in Paul's faith — faith in Christ, the faith of Christ. It led him to a new understanding of power in weakness, which he later develops in the last four chapters of 2 Corinthians. Those four chapters become the logical and fruitful outworking in his own experience and ministry of the stand that he took opposing Peter and turning away from any decree-type religion. Paul finds a new basis in the theology of the cross and the gospel of power in weakness, of which 2 Corinthians is full.

Barrett's response. It is a very true observation that compromise doesn't work, but rejecting compromise has its costs. I can think of situations in the twentieth century in which the rejection of a compromise cannot be done without paying a price. And Paul had to pay the price. I think I would like to add to it what I did not say, but about which I think most of us would agree. There are some areas in life in which you cannot do without compromise. Somebody who goes through life determined never to compromise on anything is not only going to suffer but is also going to make a whole lot of other people suffer unnecessarily. The vital, important thing is to pick out those points on which you must not compromise, whatever it costs you. I think Paul did that, and I think he was right. There are two things in the end on which he would not compromise: there had to be a mission to the Gentile world, the whole world, and there had to be no compromise with legalistic provisions.

2. Seyoon Kim reminded us of the great amount of literature produced in recent years dealing with the Jerusalem council and the incident at Antioch, especially from those who propound or who have adopted the so-called new perspective on Paul, not the least of whom is Barrett's successor at Durham, J. D. G. Dunn. The question centers on the sociological approach to Paul's doctrine of justification. At issue in justification by faith is the sociological dimension of the inclusion of the Gentiles into the body of God's

people, rather than the more fundamental question of the law and human efforts to keep the law for justification.

Barrett's response. If Professor Dunn were here he would say that my perspective — not a word I like — my view of Paul is an old-fashioned one and owes too much to a certain Martin Luther. Well, I have said what I have to say about this in an article (see the bibliography in the present volume) dealing with Paul, Luther, and Krister Stendahl's well-known essay on the introspective conscience of the West. There is a difference between Paul and Luther, but it is not the difference that Stendahl and others have found.

Barrett's relating of Stephen's party to the question of the decree reminded Kim of the whole problematic of Paul's adversaries in the various letters of Paul, but especially in 2 Corinthians. Kim called attention to an illuminating article of G. Friedrich (see the bibliography) in which he identified the opponents of Paul in 2 Corinthians as Stephen's party. Kim asked for an elaboration on questions of the Judaizing opponents of Paul, especially in Galatians, Philippians, Romans, and the Corinthian letters.

Barrett's response. Paul never mentions Stephen by name in any letter. He refers to Stephen in Acts 22, and I think that people have sometimes made too much of that. He recalls that he was present when Stephen was martyred. And people have sometimes said — I have heard it in more than one sermon — how impressed Paul was by the devotion of the martyr, by his willingness to forgive those who were killing him and so on. Of course it was impressive. And Paul cannot have witnessed it, I hope, without some impression being made. But what he is saying there, I think, is this: the Jewish authorities know perfectly well that I was an anti-Christian. I was in with those who martyred Stephen, and that shows that it was only divine intervention that sent me out on mission to the Gentile world. I think that is the line of argument in Acts 22. But that has nothing to do with the opponents of Paul in 2 Corinthians 10–13.

One further question was put by Kim. He was in agreement with Barrett that Luke in Acts is not a profound theologian as far as christology, soteriology, and the doctrine of atonement are concerned. But what about the recent widespread movement to make

him a profound salvation historical theologian? In his own way is
he not a theologian and a profound one?

Barrett's response. I do not honestly think so. I am not saying
that he has no theological convictions. Of course he has. Every
Christian has theological convictions. They may be elementary, but
there are convictions. We are believers. And belief must have some
content. Luke's belief had some content. I can think of plenty of
people far less profound in their theology than Luke. I don't want
to be misunderstood about that. He knew what he was talking
about, and he talked about what he knew. But he is not the sort
of man to say how the death of Christ saves us from our sins. How
did Christ come to be what he was? What was he before the birth
in Bethlehem? Luke doesn't drive those sorts of questions home.

3. G. Walter Hansen suggested another way of looking at the
reason Peter withdrew in Antioch. Since he was the apostle to the
circumcision (2:8), his fear of the circumcision (2:12) may have
been caused by concern for his mission to the Jews, which he felt
had now been jeopardized by his table fellowship with the Gentiles. Along the same line, Hansen asked about the feasibility of the
rather common interpretation that the decree had to do more with
mission than with salvation. The issue of salvation for the Gentiles had been decided at the Jerusalem council, but for the sake of
the mission to the circumcision, the Jews, there needed to be abstention from these certain things that were taboo because of the
teaching of the law of Moses in synagogues everywhere. When the
party from James came to Antioch, Peter felt that he would have
to make a compromise, and Paul called him on it. This compromise would not do since it was made on the basis of law and not
of Christ, and Christ must be the basis of all mission.

Paul himself seems to have been willing to make this kind of
compromise in other situations. In 1 Corinthians 8–10 he wrestles
with the same difficult problem that is addressed by the apostolic decree — that is, food offered to idols, and the accompanying
temple practices and immorality (cf. 1 Cor. 10:7–8). Here we have
the same demands of the Gentiles that were made of them in the
apostolic decree. That is, he forbids eating in the temples of idols
and immorality. He does not absolutely forbid food offered to
gods, perhaps because kosher food was unavailable in Corinth,

given the anti-Semitism we know of in Rome (cf. the decree of Claudius) and perhaps echoed in all Roman colonies. The point is that while you find Paul standing against Peter in Antioch for the compromise he made, when Paul addresses the Corinthians, who demand their freedom to eat whatever they want and to do whatever they want in the temple, Paul stops them. He thus makes some of the same demands that we see in the apostolic decree for the sake of mission.

Barrett's response. It is a most interesting suggestion that what Peter feared was that his mission to the circumcision might be injured if there was indiscriminate fellowship — unregulated fellowship — between Jewish Christians and Gentile Christians. At first examination I doubt whether it is what "fearing those of the circumcision" can be taken to mean. It is the circumcision party, I think, of which he is afraid, not of the future of his own mission. That is a first impression. I have taken it to mean, as I think most take it to mean, that here are the circumcision crowd who are getting pushy about this business, and Peter is afraid of them, afraid that they will bring him down in some way or other.

Does Paul compromise? Well of course he compromises. He says that to the Jews I became as if I were a Jew (1 Cor. 9:20). Notice the "as if I were" for a man who was born of a Jewish family circumcised on the eighth day, and all the rest of it! But I do not think that he compromised in this way. Nor do I think — although I know I am disagreeing with some recent opinion on this matter — that he compromised over *eidōlothyta,* "food offered to idols." He tells the Corinthians to buy whatever is on sale in the market and eat it. And that does not compromise with the decree.

4. From the floor it was noted that law and grace are not necessarily opposed and that the opposite to law would better be understood as lawlessness. How does faith express itself? What are the marks of those who are in the body of Christ, whether Jew or Christian?

Barrett responded that if one wants to know how faith expresses itself one could do no better than to see 1 Corinthians 13 or to note the fruit of the Spirit in Galatians 5. There are plenty of things that manifest faith, but they are not things comparable with circumcision. Paul's word is that if you are Christ's, then you are Abraham's seed, heirs in terms of the promise. That is, if you have given yourself in obedience and faith to Christ, then you are in the body, you are an heir of Abraham, you are an heir of salvation.

Hansen commented that the emphasis on the Spirit stands in opposition to circumcision in Galatians. Thus in Galatians 3 the presence of the Spirit, not circumcision, is the identifying mark of the new community. Then in chapters 5 and 6 what life in the Spirit means is spelled out in considerable detail. Certainly life in the Spirit means obligation to Christ. Martin noted that Paul even in Galatians does not quite abandon the *nomos* concept because he returns to it in chapter 6:2, "thus fulfill the law of Christ."

One questioner asked why the sabbath is not an issue mentioned in the decree of Acts 15. In response, Barrett made two points. First, it is important to see that the council, whether you follow Acts or Galatians, is not between Jews and Gentiles. These are all Jews. Titus gets in at the edge, as it were, in Galatians 2. But these are Jews considering how they are to live in the new period that has been ushered in by the life, death, and resurrection of the Messiah. Second, with very few exceptions, the sabbath does not appear as an issue in the New Testament. There is the reference in Galatians 4:10, "you observe days and months and seasons and years" (cf. Rom. 14:5), and this clearly is something that Paul does not approve of. But Paul never says to Jewish Christians, "Do not keep the sabbath," or anything like that. Martin referred to the statement in Ignatius's *Epistle to the Magnesians* 9.1, which speaks of those who "walked in ancient customs" as coming "to a new hope, no longer living for the sabbath, but for the Lord's Day."

Another speaker from the floor commented that although Paul would not compromise on the matter of salvation by faith through grace, it would not be correct to say that Paul would have understood the Jerusalem decree as defective. He is, however, sensitive to community and the importance of contextualizing for mission. Paul does not negate the right of Jews to continue practicing circumcision. They have a distinctive cultural, ethnic identity that is still valid. They are one with Gentiles in the body of Christ. But if Jews want, as Jews, to express their faith, observing Torah — not to be saved by observing Torah — to express their identity culturally, they have the right to continue to do that, as long as they do not force Torah upon the Gentiles. Gentiles do not have to become Jews, but neither do Jews have to become Gentiles.

Barrett asked this person if Jews would be right to refuse to eat together with Gentiles, if the Gentiles were not observing the dietary laws. He answered no, they should eat with Gentiles. Paul would have affirmed the Jewish people's right to continue to be Jewish in the cultural expression of their faith in the body of Christ.

Martin pointed out, however, that Paul does go on record as making the whole thing a matter of indifference. Circumcision is nothing, uncircumcision is nothing (1 Cor. 7:19; cf. Gal. 6:15). To the rejoinder that this refers to salvation, Martin replied that the issue in the passage is not salvation but a matter of "keeping the commandments of God," that is, living the Christian life.

Kim also noted Paul's statement in Romans 14:17 that "the kingdom of God is not food and drink but righteousness and peace and joy in the Holy Spirit."

Concluding Implications

The lectures of Professors Hengel and Barrett revolve around one of the most interesting and perpetually challenging issues within the New Testament: the question of continuity and discontinuity between Christianity and Judaism. The remarks that follow are ordered under these two headings.

Continuity. Of central importance in the lectures of Hengel and Barrett is the fundamental truth that Christianity has deep Jewish roots. It is hard to exaggerate the significance of this simple fact. Early Christianity was from the beginning, and for some time, exclusively and fully Jewish. With perhaps only one exception, all the writers of the New Testament were Jews who had come to faith in Jesus as the Messiah. Accordingly, a knowledge of Judaism, its history, its Scriptures and traditions, is indispensable to a correct understanding of the New Testament. For this and other reasons, Christians must learn from Jewish scholarship. This is already happening and will increase. New Testament scholars are currently rediscovering the Jewishness not only of Jesus but of Matthew and Paul too.

If the New Testament reflects Jewish thinking, albeit of a distinct kind, then the New Testament can be used as a source of knowledge about ancient Judaism. We have witnessed in the twentieth century the curious phenomenon of Jewish scholars being more conservative concerning the historical reliability of the New Testament writings than are many of their Christian counterparts. What they read of Jewish matters in the New Testament often rings true to their sense of first-century historical reality. Recently books about Paul from Jewish scholars have emphasized the Jewishness of the apostle.

All this points to the importance of mutual learning and enrichment between Jews and Christians. In particular we may again stress the lamentable ignorance of Jewish sources on the part of many Christian scholars. The importance of Jewish-Christian cooperation and dialogue is plain, not only because of the need for a more adequate scholarship and understanding of the Scriptures but also in order to combat the rising tide of secularism. Jews and Christians, for all the differences one might care to mention, must capitalize on the common ground they share and together promote the fundamental values of the Bible.

One important consequence of the thorough Jewishness of the New Testament is that hostility toward Jews and Judaism in these writings is to be regarded not as anti-Semitism but as intramural disagreement between Jews. The overheated statements of the New Testament writers against Judaism are not unlike, for example, the bitter polemic of prophets such as Isaiah against Israel. Christians today are under obligation to explain what traditional anti-Semitic texts in the New Testament do *not* mean. They furthermore must stand together with Jews against any and every manifestation of anti-Semitism. Only this can be pleasing to the Jew whom they call their Lord.

The council of Jerusalem and the controversy at Antioch in themselves point to the deep Jewish roots of Christianity. Some of the earliest Christians could not accept the implications of Paul's law-free gospel and the influx of large numbers of Gentiles into the people of God. These things did not seem consonant with the Jewish roots of these first believers. The end of the law, the people of God composed largely of Gentiles — here we encounter a surprising newness that was bound to be the cause of heated controversy. For all the proper stress that is to be put upon continuity, the confronting of the reality of discontinuity could not be avoided.

Discontinuity. No date can be established for the break between the synagogue and the church in the first century. The parting of the ways was apparently a gradual process, one that varied from place to place. According to the book of Acts as early as Stephen and the Hellenistic Jewish Christians two of the main pillars of Judaism, law and temple, began to be questioned. Obviously the destruction of Jerusalem in A.D. 70 and the consolidation of Judaism at Yavneh in the last two decades of the century were of great significance. But the falling apart and the hostility were there from a very early time and continued in a more or less steady crescendo to the end of the century and beyond.

When the gospel was preached to and accepted by growing numbers of Gentiles, Christianity was on its way to becoming a universal movement. A key issue in this transition was the question of whether these Gentile converts had to obey the Mosaic law, or, in other words, how much discontinuity with the new faith's Jewish roots would be permitted. The Jerusalem council was without question a supremely important defining moment for Christianity. Had the law been imposed on the Gentile converts, Christianity would conceivably have remained a peculiar sect within Judaism. The decision made at the council, whether involving compromise or not, validated the Gentile mission and made possible the transformation of Christianity from a Jewish to a universal movement.

Paul's letter to the Galatians is a remarkable witness to the revolution taking place in the emergence of Christianity as a universal religion. Here we read of the temporary character of the law, with its purpose now accomplished, and of the new era inaugurated by the death and resurrection of Christ. Galatians documents the transition from the law to a christocentric gospel, and thus the transition of Christianity from a manifestation of Judaism to a religion without ethnic boundaries. Here is unavoidable discontinuity with its Jewish roots, which if not affirmed would have made Christianity as we know it an impossibility.

Now, however, we must call attention to a paradox that is of the greatest importance to Paul and to all the writers of the New Testament. The undeniable discontinuity we have emphasized, when seen from a wider perspective, is an expression of what in the last analysis involves a more fundamental continuity. Thus Paul, who articulates the elements of discontinuity most forcefully, is also at pains to demonstrate that his radical gospel is the fulfillment of the Scriptures. Thus in Galatians and Romans, Paul argues that the gospel of justification by faith is exhibited already in Abraham, before and thus apart from the Mosaic law. Similarly, Paul can find the inclusion of the Gentiles in the people of God as part of the original covenant with Abraham. None of the New Testament writers would have countenanced the idea that Christianity involved a departure from or any disloyalty to the God of Israel and the faith of their fathers. The constant emphasis in the New Testament on the fulfillment of the Scriptures of Israel testifies to this.

The paradox, then, is that even the discontinuity entailed by Christianity's emergence as a universal movement is seen as foreshadowed in the Scriptures of Israel. The discontinuity is part of a larger continuity. And what of Israel's election and distinctiveness? Israel was chosen by God, but chosen for a purpose larger than itself. The early Christians regarded themselves as participating in the climax of the story of salvation that began with Israel. The Bible is not the story of God's love for Israel alone; it is the story of God's love for the whole world, and it reaches its goal in the new community established by Christ. Israel's election was not for its own sake alone but more importantly for the sake of the salvation of the world. Israel is chosen by God to be "a light to the nations" (Isa. 42:6; 49:6; cf. 60:3). And Paul, who in Romans finds the covenant faithfulness of God upheld in the remnant of Jews who have believed in the gospel, nevertheless retains the distinctiveness of Israel, to whom salvation will yet come (Rom. 11:26). And he delights in saying that "as regards election they are beloved for the sake of their forefathers. For the gifts and the call of God are irrevocable" (Rom. 11:28–29).

The motif of Israel as a light to the nations is picked up in the well-known lines of the righteous Simeon upon beholding Jesus: "Lord, now lettest thou thy servant depart in peace, according to thy word; for mine eyes have seen thy salvation which thou hast prepared in the presence of all peoples, a light for revelation to the Gentiles, and for glory to thy people Israel" (Luke 2:30–32 RSV). Israel has fulfilled its main calling in and through the Messiah Jesus. It is in this way that it has become a light to the nations. But the poignancy of the final clause can hardly be missed: "for glory to thy people Israel." It is not the fault of the Jews that Jesus has become a scandal to Israel rather than its glory. It is the fault of the church that has denied its Lord by the persecution of the Jews, and so we are back to the moving comments of Professor Hengel.

Jesus was meant to be the glory of Israel, for "salvation is from the Jews" (John 4:22). The church owes its existence to Israel: "of their race, according to the flesh, is the Christ" (Rom. 9:5). This fact should lead Christians to understand the unique relationship that they have with the Jews. This will not cancel out remaining differences, nor should it. But it should point the way to friendly relations, mutual enrichment, openness and cooperation, and dialogue that profits both sides. It has begun. Let us hope for more.

Bibliography

Barrett, C. K. *A Critical and Exegetical Commentary on the Acts of the Apostles.* 2 vols. International Critical Commentary. Edinburgh: T. & T. Clark, 1994, 1998. An exemplary commentary by a masterful commentator. Sure to become a standard for decades.

————. *Freedom and Obligation: A Study of the Epistle to the Galatians.* Philadelphia: Westminster, 1985. An exposition of Paul's gospel of freedom from the law and the conflict with Judaism and Jewish Christians.

————. "Paul and the Introspective Conscience." In *The Bible, the Reformation and the Church: Essays in Honour of James Atkinson.* Edited by W. P. Stephens. Sheffield: Academic Press, 1995, 36–48. Disagrees with the seminal essay of Krister Stendahl (noted below).

————. *Paul: An Introduction to His Thought.* Louisville: Westminster/John Knox, 1994. A fine introduction to Paul that takes the reader unfailingly to the heart of Paul's mission and theology.

Boyarin, Daniel. *A Radical Jew: Paul and the Politics of Identity.* Berkeley: University of California Press, 1994. A Jewish reading of Paul portrayed as a Jewish cultural critic.

Dunn, J. D. G. *The Partings of the Ways Between Christianity and Judaism and Their Significance for the Character of Christianity.* Philadelphia: Trinity Press International, 1991. A full and penetrating discussion of the separation of the church from the synagogue.

————, ed. *Jews and Christians: Parting of the Ways, A.D. 70–135.* Wissenschaftliche Untersuchungen zum Neuen Testament 66. Tübingen: J. C. B. Mohr, 1992; Grand Rapids: Eerdmans, 1999. Essays from the second Durham-Tübingen symposium on earliest Christianity and Judaism.

Evans, C. A., and Donald A. Hagner, eds. *Anti-Semitism and Early Christianity: Issues of Polemic and Faith.* Minneapolis: Fortress, 1993. Essays defending the conclusion that the New Testament writers and early Christianity were not anti-Semitic.

Feldmeier, R., and U. Heckel. *Die Heiden: Juden, Christen und das Problem des Fremden.* Wissenschaftliche Untersuchungen zum Neuen Testament 70. Tübingen: J. C. B. Mohr, 1994. Essays exploring how Jews and Christians have understood and interpreted their faith in new ways as the result of encounter with pagans.

Friedrich, G. "Die Gegner des Paulus im 2. Korintherbrief." In *Abraham unser Vater.* Arbeiten zum Geschichte des antiken Judentums und des Urchristentums 5. Festschrift for O. Michel. Edited by O. Betz, M. Hengel, and P. Schmidt. Leiden: E. J. Brill, 1963, 181–215.

Goulder, Michael. *St. Paul versus St. Peter: A Tale of Two Missions.* London: SCM 1994. Emphasizes greatly the differences between the perspectives of Peter and Paul and their respective followers.

Gruenwald, Ithamar. *Apocalyptic and Merkavah Mysticism.* Arbeiten zum Geschichte des antiken Judentums und des Urchristentums 14. Leiden: E. J. Brill, 1980.

Gruenwald, Ithamar, Shaul Shaked, and Gedaliahu G. Strousma, eds. *Messiah and Christos: Studies in the Jewish Origins of Christianity.* Texte und Studien zum antiken Judentum 32. Festschrift for David Flusser. Tübingen: J. C. B. Mohr, 1992.

Hagner, Donald A. *The Jewish Reclamation of Jesus: An Analysis and Critique of Modern Jewish Study of Jesus.* Grand Rapids: Zondervan, Academie Books, 1984; reprint ed., Eugene, Ore.: Wipf & Stock, 1997. A survey of twentieth-century Jewish study of Jesus arriving at the conclusion that the Jewish reclamation of Jesus has been only partially successful.

———. "Paul in Modern Jewish Thought." In *Pauline Studies. Festschrift for F. F. Bruce.* Edited by Donald A. Hagner and Murray J. Harris. Exeter: Paternoster; Grand Rapids: Eerdmans, 1980, 143–65.

Hansen, G. Walter. *Abraham in Galatians. Epistolary and Rhetorical Contexts.* Journal for the Study of the New Testament Supplement Series 29. Sheffield: JSOT, 1989. An analysis of the structure and argument of Galatians shows how Paul's interpretation of the Abraham story serves as a substructure of Pauline theology.

———. *Galatians.* InterVarsity Press New Testament Commentary. Downers Grove, Ill.: InterVarsity Press, 1994. Helpful passage-by-passage exposition of the epistle.

Hengel, Martin. *Acts and the History of Earliest Christianity.* Translated by John Bowden. Philadelphia: Fortress, 1980. A rigorous defense of the essential reliability of Acts as a historical narrative.

———. *Judaism and Hellenism: Studies in their Encounter in Palestine During the Early Hellenistic Period.* Translated by John Bowden. Philadelphia: Fortress, 1974. A classic work showing in great detail how extensively Judaism was interpenetrated by Hellenism during the Hellenistic period.

Hengel, Martin, and Anna Maria Schwemer. *Paul Between Damascus and Antioch: The Unknown Years.* Translated by John Bowden. Louisville: Westminster John Knox, 1997. A sequel to Hengel's *The Pre-Christian Paul* (Philadelphia: Trinity Press International, 1991).

Hengel, Martin, and U. Heckel, eds. *Paulus und das antike Judentum.* Tübingen: J. C. B. Mohr, 1991. Essays from the first Durham-Tübingen symposium on earliest Christianity and Judaism.

Jervell, Jacob. *The Unknown Paul. Essays on Luke-Acts and Early Christian History.* Minneapolis: Augsburg, 1984. Argues that Jewish Christianity remained of central importance to the church down to the end of the first century.

Kim, Seyoon. *The Origin of Paul's Gospel.* 2d ed. Tübingen: J. C. B. Mohr, 1984. Argues that the main elements of Paul's gospel are already made clear to Paul in his experience of the risen Christ on the Damascus road.

Klausner, Joseph. *From Jesus to Paul.* Translated by William F. Stinespring. New York: Macmillan, 1943. A brilliant Jewish study of the origins of Paul's theology.

Kohler, Kaufmann. "Saul of Tarsus." In *The Jewish Encyclopedia*. Vol. 11. Edited by Isidore Singer. New York: Funk and Wagnalls, 1905.

Lindeskog, Gösta. *Die Jesusfrage in neuzeitlichen Judentum; ein Beitrag zur Geschichte der Leben-Jesu-Forschung.* Leipzig: A. Lorentz; Uppsala: A. B. Lundquist, 1938. A pioneering, classic analysis of the Jewish study of Jesus.

Martin, Ralph P. *New Testament Foundations.* 2 vols. Grand Rapids: Eerdmans, 1986. An excellent introduction to the New Testament. Volume 2 contains material relevant to the essays in the present book.

Meissner, Stefan. *Die Heimholung des Ketzers: Studien zur jüdischen Auseinandersetzung mit Paulus.* Wissenschaftliche Untersuchungen zum Neuen Testament 2. Reihe: 87. Tübingen: J. C. B. Mohr, 1996. A thorough and excellent study of the twentieth-century Jewish reclamation of Paul.

Montefiore, C. G. *Judaism and St. Paul: Two Essays.* Reprint. New York: Arno Press, 1973. Argues that Paul's background was not rabbinic Judaism but a Hellenistically influenced Diaspora Judaism.

Rubinstein, Richard L. *My Brother Paul.* New York: Harper & Row, 1972. Affirms Paul's continuing Jewishness but looks at him primarily from the perspective of Freudian psychology.

Sandmel, Samuel. *The Genius of Paul: A Study in History.* New York: Farrar, Straus & Cudahy, 1958. The key to understanding Paul is not his Jewish but his Greek background.

Schäfer, Peter. *Hekhalot-Studien.* Texte und Studien zum antiken Judentum 19. Tübingen: J. C. B. Mohr, 1988. Studies of Jewish mysticism involving ecstatic ascent to celestial palaces and the vision of God's throne.

———. *The Hidden and Manifest God: Some Major Themes in Early Jewish Mysticism.* Translated by Aubrey Pomerance. Albany: State University of New York Press, 1992.

Schoeps, Hans Joachim. *Paul: The Theology of the Apostle in the Light of Jewish Religious History.* Translated by Harold Knight. Philadelphia: Westminster, 1961. One of the finest Jewish books on Paul. Stresses Paul's authentic, rabbinic Jewishness.

Scholem, Gershom Gerhard. *Jewish Gnosticism, Merkabah Mysticism, and Talmudic Tradition.* 2d ed. New York: Jewish Theological Seminary of America, 1965.

———. *Major Trends in Jewish Mysticism.* 3d ed. New York: Schocken, 1954. A classic treatment of the subject.

Segal, Alan F. *Paul the Convert: The Apostolate and Apostasy of Saul the Pharisee.* New Haven, Conn: Yale University Press, 1990. A brilliant study of Paul that sets him fully within a mystical, apocalyptic Judaism.

———. *Rebecca's Children: Judaism and Christianity in the Roman World.* Cambridge, Mass.: Harvard University Press, 1986. Examines the origins of both Christianity and rabbinic Judaism, and then the parting of the ways.

Stendahl, Krister. "The Apostle Paul and the Introspective Conscience of the West." First published in English in *Harvard Theological Review* 56 (1963): 199–215. Available in his collected essays, *Paul Among Jews and Gentiles,* 78–96. Philadelphia: Fortress, 1976. A much cited essay that argues that the traditional ("Lutheran") understanding of Paul is a misconstrual of the apostle and his theology. Adds stimulus to the new perspective on Paul.

Index of Ancient Sources